MOTOR OMNIBUS ROUTES IN LO

VOLUME 2

NOVEMBER 1908 - DECEMBER 1912

2nd Edition
(Completely revised and incorporating the Update published in October 1992)

LONDON HISTORICAL RESEARCH GROUP

THE OMNIBUS SOCIETY

2007

FOREWORD TO THE SECOND EDITION

The first edition of this volume was published in November 1985 and an update in the form of amendment inserts was published in October 1992. While the work continues to be a joint compilation by the Convenors of the London Historical Research Group, much of the original research was carried out by a team, all except one of whom sadly are no longer with us. Tribute must be paid to John Cummings and the late George Dawson, Mervyn Gibson, Ken Glazier, W.Noel Jackson, John King, Albert McCall, George Robbins, Bob Smyrk and Reg Westgate. Research has been ongoing and this second edition incorporates all the results of this later research and in addition has been re-formatted to bring the house style in line with recently produced volumes. A short list of amendments to Volume 1 of this work arising from this research is also included on page 3. I have been aided in preparation of this volume by the latest members of the team: Laurie Akehurst, John Bull, Dennis Cox, Chris Holland and Andrew Robertson to whom my thanks are due.

A note of any errors and omissions which are observed would be welcomed at the address at the foot of this page but please include the source of the information provided.

April 2007   David A. Ruddom

THE LONDON HISTORICAL RESEARCH GROUP
OF THE OMNIBUS SOCIETY
Meets quarterly in London and produces a quarterly Bulletin
www.omnibussoc.org

Chairman: Mr. D.A. Ruddom
Vice-Chairman: Mr. L.E. Akehurst
Hon. Secretary: Mr. J.A. Bull
***

Motor Omnibus Routes in London
Volume 1 - October 1899 to November 1908
Volume 2 - November 1908 to December 1912
Volume 3 - January 1913 to February 1915 (out of print)
Volume 4 - March 1915 to December 1919
Volume 5 - January 1920 to December 1921
Volume 6A – (LGOC routes) January 1922 to November 1924 (in preparation)
Volume 7A – (LGOC routes) December 1924 – December 1926

Available from:
L.H.R.G. Distribution Officer
57 Bluebridge Road
Brookmans Park
Hatfield, AL9 7UW

Printed by The Ludo Press Ltd, London SW17 0BA

ISBN-13: 978 0 901307 69 9
ISBN-10: 0 901307 69 6

AMENDMENTS TO VOLUME 1 (Revised Edition)

Page 36 London General Omnibus Company
Add:

?.03.07	Daily	Barnes (White Hart) – Liverpool Street service and the Barnes (White Hart) – Oxford Circus service extended daily from Barnes (White Hart) to operate from Barnes (Avondale Road) due to traffic congestion at the White Hart stand. *Tickets described this as Mortlake (Avondale Road). Some sources suggest Mortlake Green (opposite the White Hart) continued to be used as an overflow for the Avondale Road stand.*

Pages 36, 40, 42, 44, 47, 50, 54, 59 and 62 London General Omnibus Company
Amend all references to Barnes (White Hart) apart from the above to read: Barnes (Avondale Road).

Page 51 London and North Western Railway Company
Add:

.04.08	Weekdays	New Service: Watford Junction Station – Bushey Heath (Three Crowns) via Clarendon Road†, Market Place, Watford High Street, Bushey Station, Chalk Hill, London Road, High Street Bushey, Sparrows Herne. † one evening journey operates via Queens Road instead of Clarendon Road.

Page 55 London and North Western Railway Company
Add after the Watford Junction – Croxley Green and Watford Junction – Harrow Station routes:
                               via Queens Road.
Add:

	Weekdays	Watford Junction Station – Bushey Heath (Three Crowns) via Clarendon Road

London & North Western Railway

Page 57 London and North Western Railway Company
Add:

By 07.08	Weekdays	The Watford Junction – Harrow Station and Watford Junction – Bushey Heath routes merged so that most journeys operate via Queens Road with only three southbound and four northbound journeys operating via Clarendon Road.

London & North Western Railway

Page 57 London Road-Car Route K
01.07.08 Delete Effra Road, Water Lane and substitute Railton Road.

Page 57 London and North Western Railway Company
Add after the 13.07.08 entry for the Watford Junction – Harrow Station extension:
                               Peterborough Road, High Street Harrow on the Hill. *See also the note on page 9 of this volume regarding the method of operation of this route.*

Page 57 London Road-Car Route K
27.07.08 Delete Effra Road and substitute Atlantic Road.

Page 63 London General Omnibus Company
Route 20 Delete Effra Road, Water Lane, Dulwich Road and substitute Atlantic Road, Railton Road.

Page 64 London and North Western Railway Company
Amend the via points on the Watford Junction – Harrow (Post Office) route to read:
                               via Queens Road (some journeys via Clarendon Road, Market Place), High Street…..

INTRODUCTION

This volume commences with a complete list of routes as at 2nd November 1908, the finishing point of Volume 1. Thereafter, there are two full lists for each year, one showing the winter services, usually in January and the other, the fullest summer services, normally around the August Bank Holiday. In between are the lists of alterations and new services, in chronological order. Where appropriate and possible they are cross-referenced when they affect more than one route.

As will be seen, this was a period of rapid development for the motor bus. Horse bus routes were steadily disappearing as the internal combustion engine took over. The first public L.G.O.C. list of routes was dated April 1910 - it contained details of motor bus routes 1 - 24 (less number 13), two of which, 18 and 23, were Sunday only operations. It also contains details of no less than 37 horse bus routes still operating. The first map and guide was dated March 1911 and by this time only ten horse operated services were listed and the last of these - the 32 from Moorgate to London Bridge - ran its final journey on 25th October 1911, although some other operators continued to favour animal power. Other events of note include the first L.G.O.C. single deck bus route - the 69 in November 1912, which was also the first motor bus to run through the Blackwall Tunnel and relieved the horses of the Tilling service from their thankless task in the gloom. In December 1912 came the first use of a suffix to a route number when the 35A was commenced as a bifurcation in Walthamstow of the 35.

A great deal of research has been done into contemporary press reports, etc., and it is not possible for reasons of space to include details of sources. Reference has been made to the Reports of the London Traffic Branch of the Board of Trade in 1908, 1909, 1910, 1911 and 1912, which contain considerable detail but only on specific dates when the lists of routes were prepared. However, they are useful for confirming routeings and terminals.

With regard to the L.G.O.C. Map and Guides, which were published monthly until the First World War intervened, experience has shown that in certain instances these were not necessarily exact. Where the information recorded here differs from that shown in these maps and guides, it can be assumed as correct, wherever other offical contemporary records have been available. Examples of this are the 86 route which is shown in the September 1912 map as operating through from North Woolwich to Barkingside. This never happened as the dock bridges were not available for buses at that date. Also on the same September 1912 map the 50 is shown as diverted to Ealing Broadway and new routes 62 Victoria Station to Plumstead, 90 Hammersmith Broadway to Richmond, 91 Ealing Broadway to Kew Bridge and 92 Hounslow Barracks Station to Virginia Water are quoted but no proof has been found that any of these ever operated although 91 did commence on 2nd December 1912. Indeed 62 seems to have been a very speculative number since it was listed as 'Wanstead - North Woolwich to be started shortly' in the October 1912 map but again did not materialise. Again, by December 1912 the potential service to North Woolwich was being promulgated prematurely as Route 71. However, as will be seen in Volume 3, it was not until 8th May 1913 that a service was provided over the dock bridges to North Woolwich and then it was numbered 54.

D.A.Ruddom
Brookmans Park
2007

DESCRIPTION OF TERMINAL POINTS

One of the problems in compiling this series of books is the changing description of various terminal points that have occurred over the years. To quote two examples, what we now recognise as 'Swiss Cottage' was described originally as 'St. John's Wood (Swiss Cottage)', then 'South Hampstead (Swiss Cottage)' , sometimes as 'Swiss Cottage (Eton Avenue) and at others simply as 'South Hampstead'. Buses turning at Mortlake Garage for many years displayed 'Barnes (Avondale Road)'. This changed for a period to 'Barnes (Mortlake L.G.O.C. Garage)', then became plain 'Mortlake' and now with the demise of the actual garage we have 'Mortlake (Avondale Road)'.

This section is an attempt to explain what may appear as inconsistencies between this particular volume and the various volumes of this series. In addition there are some cases where the editors have adopted a policy of using a uniform description for what is plainly one location but which may have a variety of stand points in the immediate vicinity.

Barnes (Avondale Road)
: This has also been described as Barnes (Mortlake L.G.O.C. Garage) and in the 1930s became described as Mortlake although early tickets used Mortlake rather than Barnes ini contradiction with contemporary maps and destinations on vehicles. With the demise of Mortlake Garage in 1983 the continuing terminal is described as Mortlake (Avondale Road).

Camden Town Station (Und.)
: In addition to Camden Town Station (Und.) the various termini around this point, which included stands in Greenland Road and Bayham Street, have also been described as 'Britannia' and 'Old Mother Red Cap' both of which are on opposite corners of the main junction by the Underground station. The Camden Gardens stand is however considered to be sufficiently removed from the Underground Station and the description Camden Town (Camden Gardens) is used to show this terminal.

Chalk Farm (Adelaide)
: This is the contemporary name for this volume of the terminus which is synonymous with Chalk Farm (Enterprise) and Chalk Farm Station (Und.).

Clapham Common Station (Und.)
: Stands were at Venn Street and Old Town and passengers were carried to and from these. The generic term is used however although changes between the stands are recorded where they occur.

Cranbrook Park
: This is the terminal referred to in modern parlance as Gants Hill Station. Originally qualified by Beehive Lane, this was later changed to Eastern Avenue when that road was built.

Cricklewood (L.G.O.C. Garage)
: Contemporary documents cite this as Dollis Hill (Cricklewood L.G.O.C. Garage) but the Dollis Hill name was subsequently dropped.

Fulham (Salisbury)
: Metropolitan Steam and National Steam terminals at Walham Green. Metropolitan used the name 'Walham Green' for their terminal. It had been assumed that this referred to Walham Green (now Fulham Broadway) Station on the District Railway, or its near vicinity. National used Fulham 'The Salisbury', which is in Dawes Road, approximately ¼ mile west of Walham Green Station. Research in local press reports and in the annual reports of the Traffic Branch of the Board of Trade has confirmed that the Metropolitan's 'Walham Green' was, in fact, also 'The Salisbury' and this name is used throughout this volume.

Pimlico (Gun)
: This concerns Route 24. The terminus was originally quoted as The Gun Tavern which stood on the north west corner of Glasgow Terrace and Lupus Street and buses traversed the anti-clockwise loop shown in the route description on page 52. On 21.05.1914 as shown in Volume 3 this changed to a clockwise loop and later the terminus is described in contemporary records as both Pimlico (Grosvenor Road) and Pimlico (Waterman's Steps) which was on Grosvenor Road. The present day anti-clockwise terminal working was introduced in 1927 when the stand was moved to the William IV public house on Grosvenor Road. Note too that Glasgow Terrace today follows a completely different alignment from that at the time of this volume.

St. Albans (Rising Sun)   This is the term in use during the period of this volume although later records show St. Albans (Market Place). The 'Rising Sun', long since disappeared, was at No.15 St. Peter's Street immediately to the south of the alleyway leading through to Waddington Road. Strictly speaking this means the routes terminated in St. Peter's Street rather than Market Place but this section of road is usually considered to be part of the Market Place (and is still so used). The one way anti-clockwise working contemporary with this volume via Chequer Street and Market Place, High Street was not worked on market days when buses went both ways via Chequer Street.

Seven Kings (Seven Kings Hotel   The Seven Kings Hotel was adjacent to the garage which was not opened until 08.05.1913 (see Volume 3) and at the time of this volume buses turned on the hotel forecourt.

Shoreditch Church   This terminal is also cited at times as 'George and Dragon' and 'Calvert Avenue'. These are adjacent to the church which for many years has been the recognised name for this point.

South Hampstead (Swiss Cottage)   This terminal was originally called 'St. John's Wood (Swiss Cottage)' and was also referred to as 'Swiss Cottage (Eton Avenue)'. During the 1930s it became cited as plain 'Swiss Cottage'.

Stratford Broadway   In early years this was sometimes quoted as Stratford (Swan) which was at the western end of the Broadway by the top of West Ham Lane. In later years buses circumnavigated the church and so the general term Stratford Broadway has been adopted.

Victoria Station   The traditional terminus at Victoria was the station forecourt but in later years independent operators and also L.G.O.C. after taking over such routes used Buckingham Palace Road.

West Hendon (Station Road)   This was the description used by L.G.O.C. and in some volumes of this work. However, since this terminal is nowadays known as 'West Hendon' this description has been adopted to clarify at which end of Station Road routes like the 83 are terminating.

Wimbledon (Rose & Crown)   This was described thus in contemporary L.G.O.C. publicity although more correctly it should be described as Wimbledon Common (Rose & Crown). The area is also known as Wimbledon Village.

MOTOR OMNIBUS ROUTES AS AT MONDAY 2ND NOVEMBER 1908

(a) L.G.O.C.

This was the date on which the L.G.O.C. introduced numbers on all routes. Some vehicles of Vanguard and the London Road-Car retained their original liveries for some time after this date.

No	Operation	Route	Formerly
1	Daily	Cricklewood (Crown) - Elephant & Castle via Cricklewood Broadway, Shoot-Up Hill, Kilburn High Road, Maida Vale, Edgware Road, Chapel Street, Marylebone Road*, Euston Road, Tottenham Court Road, Charing Cross Road, St. Martin's Place, Duncannon Street, Strand, Wellington Street*, Waterloo Bridge, Waterloo Road.	Vanguard 1 & L.G.O.C.
2	Daily	Ebury Bridge (Monster) – Childs Hill (Castle) via Warwick Street, Wilton Road, Victoria Street, Grosvenor Gardens (north side), Grosvenor Place, Hyde Park Corner, Hamilton Place, Park Lane, Marble Arch, Oxford Street, Orchard Street, Portman Square (east side), Baker Street, York Place*, Upper Baker Street*, Park Road, Wellington Road, Finchley Road.	Vanguard 2
3	Daily	Oxford Circus - South Croydon (Swan & Sugar Loaf) via Regent Street, Piccadilly Circus, Haymarket, Cockspur Street, Whitehall, Parliament Street, Bridge Street, Westminster Bridge, Westminster Bridge Road, Kennington Road, Kennington Park Road, Brixton Road, Brixton Hill, Streatham Hill, Streatham High Road, London Road, North End, High Street Croydon, South End, Brighton Road.	Vanguard 3
4	Daily	Shepherds Bush (Bush Hotel) - Herne Hill (Half Moon Hotel) via Shepherds Bush Road, Brook Green Road*, Hammersmith Broadway, Fulham Palace Road, High Street Fulham, Putney Bridge, High Street Putney, Upper Richmond Road, West Hill, High Street Wandsworth, East Hill, St. Johns Hill, St. Johns Road, Battersea Rise, Clapham Common North Side, The Pavement, Clapham Park Road, Acre Lane, Effra Road, Water Lane, Dulwich Road.	Vanguard 4
5		*Number not in use.*	
6	Weekdays Sundays	Kensal Rise Station - Liverpool Street Station Kensal Rise Station – Charing Cross (Trafalgar Square) via Station Road*, Chamberlayne Road, Kilburn Lane, Canterbury Road*, Malvern Road*, Shirland Road, Formosa Street, Warwick Avenue, Clifton Gardens, Maida Vale, Edgware Road, Marble Arch, Oxford Street, Regent Street, Piccadilly Circus, Haymarket, Cockspur Street, Trafalgar Square (south side), Strand, Fleet Street, Ludgate Hill, St. Paul's Churchyard, Cannon Street, Queen Victoria Street, Princes Street, Moorgate Street, London Wall, Blomfield Street, Liverpool Street (return via New Broad Street*, Old Broad Street, Threadneedle Street).	Vanguard 6
7	Daily	Wormwood Scrubs (Pavilion) - Liverpool Street Station via North Pole Road, St. Quintin Avenue, St. Mark's Road, Cambridge Gardens, Ladbroke Grove, Cornwall Road*, Richmond Road*, Westbourne Grove, Bishops Road*, Eastbourne Terrace, Praed Street, Edgware Road, Marble Arch, Oxford Street, New Oxford Street, High Holborn, Holborn, Holborn Viaduct, Newgate Street, Cheapside, Bank, Princes Street, Moorgate Street, London Wall, Blomfield Street, Liverpool Street (return via New Broad Street*, Old Broad Street, Threadneedle Street).	Vanguard 7 & Road-Car J
8	Daily	Shepherds Bush (Bush Hotel) - Seven Kings (Seven Kings Hotel) via Uxbridge Road, Holland Park Avenue, High Street Notting Hill Gate*, Bayswater Road, Marble Arch, Oxford Street, New Oxford Street, High Holborn, Holborn, Holborn Viaduct, Newgate Street, Cheapside, Bank, Cornhill, Leadenhall Street, Aldgate, Aldgate High Street, Whitechapel High Street, Whitechapel Road, Mile End Road, Bow Road, Stratford High Street, Stratford Broadway, Romford Road, Ilford Hill, Ilford High Road, Seven Kings High Road.	Vanguard 8 & L.G.O.C.

9	Weekdays Sundays	Hammersmith Broadway – Shoreditch Church Kew Green (Coach & Horses) - Shoreditch Church via Kew Bridge, Chiswick High Road, King Street, Hammersmith Broadway, Hammersmith Road, Kensington Road*, Kensington High Street, Kensington Road, Kensington Gore, Knightsbridge, Hyde Park Corner, Piccadilly, Piccadilly Circus, Lower Regent Street, Waterloo Place, Pall Mall, Cockspur Street, Trafalgar Square (south side), Strand, Fleet Street, Ludgate Hill, St. Paul's Churchyard, Cannon Street, Queen Victoria Street, Bank, Threadneedle Street, Bishopsgate Street*, Norton Folgate, Shoreditch High Street.	Road-Car L
10	Daily	Elephant & Castle - Leytonstone (Green Man) via Newington Causeway, Borough High Street, London Bridge, Gracechurch Street, Fenchurch Street, Aldgate, Aldgate High Street, Whitechapel High Street, Whitechapel Road, Mile End Road, Bow Road, Stratford High Street, Stratford Broadway, The Grove, Maryland Point, Leytonstone Road, Leytonstone High Road.	Vanguard 10
11	Daily	Liverpool Street Station – Barnes (Avondale Road) via New Broad Street*, Old Broad Street, Threadneedle Street (return via Princes Street, Moorgate Street*, London Wall, Blomfield Street, Liverpool Street), Bank, Queen Victoria Street, Cannon Street, St. Paul's Churchyard, Ludgate Hill, Fleet Street, Strand, Charing Cross, Whitehall, Parliament Street, Parliament Square, Broad Sanctuary, Victoria Street, Buckingham Palace Road, Pimlico Road, Lower Sloane Street, Sloane Square, Kings Road, Harwood Road, The Broadway Walham Green*, Jerdan Place, Dawes Road, Crown Road*, Fulham Palace Road, Queen Street*, Hammersmith Bridge Road, Hammersmith Bridge, Castelnau, Church Road, Barnes High Street, Barnes Terrace*.	L.G.O.C.
12		*Number not in use.*	
13	Weekdays Sundays	Shoreditch Church – Hammersmith Broadway Charing Cross (Trafalgar Square) - Putney Station via Shoreditch High Street, Norton Folgate, Bishopsgate Street*, Threadneedle Street, Bank, Queen Victoria Street, Cannon Street, St. Paul's Churchyard, Ludgate Hill, Fleet Street, Strand, Trafalgar Square (south side), Cockspur Street, Haymarket, Piccadilly Circus, Regent Street, Oxford Street, Marble Arch, Bayswater Road, High Street Notting Hill Gate*, Holland Park Avenue, Goldhawk Road*, Shepherds Bush Road, Brook Green Road*, Hammersmith Broadway, Queen Street*, Fulham Palace Road, Fulham High Street, Putney Bridge, Putney High Street.	Road-Car S
14	Daily	Putney Station - Stratford Broadway via Putney High Street, Putney Bridge, Fulham High Street, Fulham Road, The Broadway Walham Green*, Fulham Road, Sydney Place, Onslow Square, Thurloe Place, Brompton Road, Knightsbridge, Hyde Park Corner, Piccadilly, Piccadilly Circus, Haymarket (?), Cockspur Street, Trafalgar Square (south side), Strand, Fleet Street, Ludgate Hill, St. Paul's Churchyard, Cannon Street, Queen Victoria Street, Bank, Cornhill, Leadenhall Street, Aldgate, Aldgate High Street, Whitechapel High Street, Whitechapel Road, Mile End Road, Bow Road, Stratford High Street.	Road-Car T
15	Daily	Shepherds Bush (Bush Hotel) - East Ham (Duke's Head) via Uxbridge Road, Holland Park Avenue, High Street Notting Hill Gate*, Bayswater Road, Marble Arch, Oxford Street, New Oxford Street, High Holborn, Holborn, Holborn Viaduct, Newgate Street, Cheapside, Bank, Cornhill, Leadenhall Street, Aldgate, Aldgate High Street, Whitechapel High Street, Commercial Road East*, East India Dock Road, Barking Road.	Road-Car C & L.G.O.C.
16	Daily	Victoria Station - Cricklewood (Crown) via Wilton Road, Victoria Street (return via Buckingham Palace Road), Grosvenor Gardens (north side), Grosvenor Place, Hyde Park Corner, Hamilton Place, Park Lane, Marble Arch, Edgware Road, Maida Vale, Kilburn High Road, Shoot-Up Hill, Cricklewood Broadway.	L.G.O.C.

17	Daily	Ealing Broadway (Railway Hotel) - Plaistow (Abbey Arms) via Ealing Broadway, The Mall, Uxbridge Road, Acton High Street, Acton Vale, Uxbridge Road, Holland Park Avenue, High Street Notting Hill Gate*, Bayswater Road, Marble Arch, Oxford Street, New Oxford Street, High Holborn, Holborn, Holborn Viaduct, Newgate Street, Cheapside, Bank, Cornhill, Leadenhall Street, Aldgate, Aldgate High Street, Whitechapel High Street, Commercial Road East*, East India Dock Road, Barking Road.	L.G.O.C.
18	Daily	Leyton (Bakers Arms) - Oxford Circus via Lea Bridge Road, Lower Clapton Road, Mare Street, Cambridge Road*, Bethnal Green Road, Shoreditch High Street, Norton Folgate, Bishopsgate Street*, Threadneedle Street, Bank, Cheapside, Newgate Street, Holborn Viaduct, Holborn, High Holborn, New Oxford Street, Oxford Street.	L.G.O.C.
19	Daily	Clapham Junction (Northcote) – Highbury Barn (Tavern) via St. John's Road, Falcon Road, Battersea Park Road, Battersea Bridge Road, Battersea Bridge, Beaufort Street, Kings Road, Sloane Square, Sloane Street, Knightsbridge, Hyde Park Corner, Piccadilly, Piccadilly Circus, Shaftesbury Avenue, Charing Cross Road, New Oxford Street, Hart Street*, Vernon Place, Theobalds Road, Rosebery Avenue, St. John Street, Islington High Street, Upper Street, St. Paul's Road, Highbury Grove.	Road-Car H
20	Daily	Hammersmith Broadway - Tulse Hill (Tulse Hill Hotel) via Brook Green Road* , Shepherds Bush Road, Netherwood Road, Richmond Road*, Holland Park Avenue, High Street Notting Hill Gate*, Bayswater Road, Marble Arch, Oxford Street, Regent Street, Piccadilly Circus, Lower Regent Street(?), Waterloo Place(?), Pall Mall(?), Cockspur Street, Whitehall, Parliament Street, Parliament Square, Broad Sanctuary, Great Smith Street, Marsham Street, Earl Street*, Page Street, Grosvenor Road*, Vauxhall Bridge, South Lambeth Road, Stockwell Road, Brixton Road, Atlantic Road, Railton Road, Dulwich Road, Norwood Road.	Road-Car K

 (b) Other Operators

      (i)   General Motor Cab Company *[route was not numbered]*

      Daily   Earls Court - Portland Place (express service).

      (ii)   Great Eastern London Motor Omnibus Company *[routes were not numbered]*

      Daily   Shepherds Bush - Ilford Broadway
        via Uxbridge Road, Holland Park Avenue, High Street Notting Hill Gate*, Bayswater Road, Marble Arch, Oxford Street, New Oxford Street, High Holborn, Holborn, Holborn Viaduct, Newgate Street, Cheapside, Bank, Cornhill, Leadenhall Street, Aldgate, Aldgate High Street, Whitechapel High Street, Whitechapel Road, Mile End Road, Bow Road, Stratford High Street, Stratford Broadway, Romford Road, Ilford Hill.

      Weekdays Leyton (Bakers' Arms) – Elephant & Castle
      Sundays   Epping Forest (Rising Sun) – Elephant & Castle
        via Woodford New Road, Forest Rise, Whipps Cross, Lea Bridge Road, Lower Clapton Road, Mare Street, Cambridge Road*, Bethnal Green Road, Shoreditch High Street, Norton Folgate, Bishopsgate Street*, Gracechurch Street, London Bridge, Borough High Street, Newington Causeway.

      Weekdays Leyton (Bakers' Arms) – Oxford Circus
      Sundays   Epping Forest (Rising Sun) – Marble Arch
        via Woodford New Road, Forest Rise, Whipps Cross, Lea Bridge Road, Lower Clapton Road, Mare Street, Cambridge Road*, Bethnal Green Road, Shoreditch High Street, Norton Folgate, Bishopsgate Street*, Threadneedle Street, Bank, Cheapside, Newgate Street, Holborn Viaduct, Holborn, High Holborn, New Oxford Street, Oxford Street.

Daily	Leytonstone (Green Man) - Elephant & Castle via Leytonstone High Road, Leytonstone Road, Maryland Point, The Grove, Stratford Broadway, Stratford High Street, Bow Road, Mile End Road, Whitechapel Road, Whitechapel High Street, Aldgate High Street, Aldgate, Fenchurch Street, Gracechurch Street, London Bridge, Borough High Street, Newington Causeway.
Weekdays Sundays	Upton Park – Charing Cross (Trafalgar Square) Upton Park – Marble Arch via Barking Road, East India Dock Road, Commercial Road, Whitechapel High Street, Aldgate High Street, Aldgate, Leadenhall Street, Cornhill, Bank, Queen Victoria Street Cannon Street, St. Paul's Churchyard, Ludgate Hill, Fleet Street, Strand, Trafalgar Square (south side), Cockspur Street, Haymarket(?), Piccadilly Circus, Regent Street, Oxford Street

(iii)   <u>London and North Western Railway</u> *[routes were not numbered]*

Weekdays	Watford Junction Station - Croxley Green (Yorke Road) via Woodford Road, Queens Road, Watford High Street, Market Place, Market Street, Cassio Road, Whippendell Road, Harwoods Road, Rickmansworth Road, Watford Road.
Weekdays	Watford Junction Station - Harrow & Wealdstone Station via Queens Road, (some journeys via Clarendon Road, Market Place), Watford High Street, Lower High Street, Pinner Road, Aldenham Road, Chalk Hill, London Road, High Street Bushey, Sparrows Herne, High Road Bushey Heath, Common Road, Brooks Hill, Chapel Hill Road*, High Road Harrow Weald, Wealdstone High Street.
Weekdays	Harrow & Wealdstone Station – Harrow (Post Office) via Station Road, Peterborough Road, High Street Harrow on the Hill. *[NOTE: Although advertised as a separate service, through fares from the Watford route were available and most buses worked through from Watford to Harrow (Post Office) with varying waits at Harrow & Wealdstone Station depending on train arrivals and departures]*

(iv)   <u>London Central Motor Omnibus Company</u> *[route was not numbered]*

Daily	Chalk Farm (Adelaide) - Camberwell Green via Chalk Farm Road, Camden Town High Street*, Seymour Street*, Eversholt Street, Upper Woburn Place, Tavistock Square, Woburn Place, Russell Square (east side), Southampton Row, Kingsway, Aldwych (western arm), Wellington Street*, Waterloo Bridge, Waterloo Road, London Road, Elephant & Castle, Walworth Road*, Camberwell Road.

(v)   <u>London Electrobus Company</u> *[route was not numbered]*

Daily	Victoria Station - Liverpool Street Station via Wilton Road (return via Victoria Street, Buckingham Palace Road), Victoria Street, Broad Sanctuary, Parliament Square, Parliament Street, Whitehall, Charing Cross, Strand, Fleet Street, Ludgate Hill, St. Paul's Churchyard, Cannon Street, Queen Victoria Street, Bank, Princes Street, Moorgate Street*, London Wall, Blomfield Street, Liverpool Street (return via New Broad Street*, Old Broad Street, Threadneedle Street).

(vi)   <u>Metropolitan Steam Omnibus Company</u> *[routes were not numbered]*

Daily	Barnes (Red Lion) - Piccadilly Circus via Castelnau, Hammersmith Bridge, Hammersmith Bridge Road, Queen Street*, Hammersmith Broadway, Hammersmith Road, Kensington Road*, Kensington High Street, Kensington Road, Kensington Gore, Knightsbridge, Hyde Park Corner, Piccadilly.

(vii)   F.Newman   *[route was not numbered]*

Daily   Peckham (Rye Lane) - Marylebone Station
                  via Peckham High Street, Peckham Road, Church Street*, Camberwell Green,
                  Camberwell Road, Walworth Road*, Elephant & Castle, St. George's Road,
                  Westminster Bridge Road, Westminster Bridge, Bridge Street, Parliament
                  Street, Whitehall, Cockspur Street, Pall Mall, Waterloo Place, Lower Regent
                  Street, Piccadilly Circus, Regent Street, Oxford Street, Orchard Street, Portman
                  Square (east side), Baker Street, York Place*, Marylebone Road.

(viii) Thomas Tilling

Daily   Sidcup (Black Horse) - Oxford Circus
                  via Sidcup High Street, Foots Cray Road*, Victoria Road*, Eltham High
                  Street, Eltham Hill, Eltham Green, Eltham Road, Lee High Road, Lee Bridge,
                  Lewisham High Street, Loampit Vale, Loampit Hill, Lewisham High Road*,
                  New Cross Road, Queens Road, Peckham High Street, Peckham Road, Church
                  Street*, Camberwell Green, Camberwell Road, Walworth Road*, Elephant &
                  Castle, St. George's Road, Westminster Bridge Road, Westminster Bridge,
                  Bridge Street, Parliament Street, Whitehall, Cockspur Street, Pall Mall,
                  Waterloo Place, Lower Regent Street, Piccadilly Circus, Regent Street

Daily   Catford (Rushey Green) – Peckham (Rye Lane)
                  via Rushey Green, Lewisham High Street, Loampit Vale, Loampit Hill,
                  Lewisham High Road*, New Cross Road, Queens Road, Peckham High Street.

Daily   Peckham (Rye Lane) - Oxford Circus
                  via Peckham High Street, Peckham Road, Church Street*, Camberwell Green,
                  Camberwell Road, Walworth Road*, Elephant & Castle, St. George's Road,
                  Westminster Bridge Road, Westminster Bridge, Bridge Street, Parliament
                  Street, Whitehall, Cockspur Street, Pall Mall, Waterloo Place, Lower Regent
                  Street, Piccadilly Circus, Regent Street.

ALTERATIONS FROM 2ND NOVEMBER 1908 TO 31ST JANUARY 1909

NOTE: No record of the services operated on Christmas Day or Boxing Day, 25/26.12.1908 has
been seen.

(a) L.G.O.C.

06.12.1908	9	Daily	Last day of operation on Sundays between Kew Green and Turnham Green Church.
10.12.1908	9	Daily	Extended on Mondays to Saturdays from Shoreditch Church to Leyton (Bakers' Arms) via Hackney Road, Cambridge Road*, Mare Street, Lower Clapton Road, Lea Bridge Road.
10.12.1908	12	Daily	New Route: Turnham Green (Church) - Ilford Broadway via Chiswick High Road, Goldhawk Road*, Holland Park Avenue, High Street Notting Hill Gate*, Bayswater Road, Marble Arch, Oxford Street, New Oxford Street, High Holborn, Holborn, Holborn Viaduct, Newgate Street, Cheapside, Bank, Cornhill, Leadenhall Street, Aldgate, Aldgate High Street, Whitechapel High Street, Whitechapel Road, Mile End Road, Bow Road, Stratford High Street, Stratford Broadway, Romford Road, Ilford Hill.
31.12.1908	5	Daily	New Route: Chalk Farm (Adelaide) - Camberwell Green via Chalk Farm Road, Camden Town High Street*, Seymour Street*, Eversholt Street, Upper Woburn Place, Tavistock Square, Woburn Place, Russell Square (east side), Southampton Row, Kingsway, Aldwych (western arm), Wellington Street*, Waterloo Bridge, Waterloo Road, London Road, Elephant & Castle, Walworth Road*, Camberwell Road.
13.01.1909	13	Daily	Last day of operation (see 6, 12).

11

| 14.01.1909 | 6 | Daily | Withdrawn between Bank and Liverpool Street Station and re-routed on Mondays to Saturdays to operate to Shoreditch Church via Threadneedle Street, Bishopsgate Street*, Norton Folgate, Shoreditch High Street. (see 13). |

(b) Other Operators

      (i)   Great Eastern London Motor Omnibus Company Ltd.

...11.1908	Daily	Leytonstone (Green Man) - Elephant & Castle route withdrawn between Leytonstone (Green Man) and Stratford Broadway.
15.11.1908	Daily	Epping Forest - Marble Arch route withdrawn on Sundays between Epping Forest (Rising Sun) and Leyton (Bakers' Arms).
17.12.1908	Daily	Shepherds Bush - Ilford Broadway route withdrawn between Shepherds Bush and Marble Arch and re-routed to operate daily from West Kilburn (Falcon) via Shirland Road, Formosa Street, Warwick Avenue, Clifton Gardens, Maida Vale, Edgware Road to Marble Arch and line of route.

      (ii)   F.Newman

| By 23.01.1909 | Daily | Peckham (Rye Lane) - Marylebone Station route withdrawn between Oxford Circus and Marylebone Station. |

MOTOR OMNIBUS ROUTES AS AT SUNDAY 31ST JANUARY 1909

(i)   L.G.O.C.

1	Daily	Cricklewood (Crown) - Elephant & Castle
2	Daily	Ebury Bridge (Monster) - Childs Hill (Castle)
3	Daily	Oxford Circus - South Croydon (Swan & Sugar Loaf)
4	Daily	Shepherds Bush (Bush Hotel) - Herne Hill (Half Moon Hotel)
5	Daily	Chalk Farm (Adelaide) - Camberwell Green
6	Weekdays	Kensal Rise Station - Shoreditch Church
	Sundays	Kensal Rise Station - Charing Cross (Trafalgar Square)
7	Daily	Wormwood Scrubs - Liverpool Street Station
8	Daily	Shepherds Bush (Bush Hotel) - Seven Kings (Seven Kings Hotel)
9	Weekdays	Hammersmith Broadway - Leyton (Bakers' Arms)
	Sundays	Turnham Green Church - Shoreditch Church
10	Daily	Elephant & Castle - Leytonstone (Green Man)
11	Daily	Liverpool Street Station - Barnes (Avondale Road)
12	Daily	Turnham Green Church - Ilford Broadway
13		*Number not in use*
14	Daily	Putney Station - Stratford Broadway
15	Daily	Shepherds Bush (Bush Hotel) - East Ham (Dukes Head)
16	Daily	Victoria Station - Cricklewood (Crown)
17	Daily	Ealing Broadway (Railway Hotel) - Plaistow (Abbey Arms)

18	Daily	Leyton (Bakers' Arms) - Oxford Circus
19	Daily	Clapham Junction (Northcote) - Highbury Barn (Tavern)
20	Daily	Hammersmith Broadway - Tulse Hill (Tulse Hill Hotel)

(b) Other Operators

(i) General Motor Cab Company

Daily Earls Court - Portland Place (express service)

(ii) Great Eastern London Motor Omnibus Company Ltd.

Daily West Kilburn (Falcon) - Ilford Broadway

Weekdays Leyton (Bakers' Arms) - Elephant & Castle
Sundays Epping Forest (Rising Sun) - Elephant & Castle

Weekdays Leyton (Bakers' Arms) - Oxford Circus
Sundays Leyton (Bakers' Arms) - Marble Arch

Daily Stratford Broadway - Elephant & Castle

Weekdays Upton Park - Charing Cross (Trafalgar Square)
Sundays Upton Park - Marble Arch

(iii) London and North Western Railway Company

Weekdays Watford Junction Station - Croxley Green (Yorke Road)

Weekdays Watford Junction Station - Harrow & Wealdstone Station

Weekdays Harrow & Wealdstone Station – Harrow (Post Office)

(iv) London Central Omnibus Company Ltd.

Daily Chalk Farm (Adelaide) - Camberwell Green

(v) London Electrobus Company Ltd.

Daily Victoria Station - Liverpool Street Station

(vi) Metropolitan Steam Omnibus Company Ltd.

Daily Barnes (Red Lion) - Piccadilly Circus

(vii) F.Newman

Daily Peckham (Rye Lane) - Oxford Circus

(viii) Thomas Tilling Ltd.

Daily Sidcup (Black Horse) - Oxford Circus

Daily Catford (Rushey Green) - Peckham (Rye Lane)

Daily Peckham (Rye Lane) - Oxford Circus

ALTERATIONS FROM 1ST FEBRUARY 1909 TO 2ND AUGUST 1909

NOTE: Public holidays during this period on which Sunday services usually operated were 09.04.1909 (Good Friday), 12.04.1909 (Easter Monday), 31.05.1909 (Whit Monday) and 02.08.1909 (August Bank Holiday).

(a)   L.G.O.C.

22.02.1909	18	Daily	Extended on weekdays from Oxford Circus to West Kilburn (Falcon) via Oxford Street, Marble Arch, Edgware Road, Maida Vale, Clifton Gardens, Warwick Avenue, Formosa Street, Shirland Road, Malvern Road*.
11.03.1909			*West Norwood garage (U) opened.*
04.04.1909	18	Daily	Additional Sunday service introduced under this number: Buckhurst Hill (Bald Faced Stag) - Bethnal Green (Green Man) via High Road Buckhurst Hill, Woodford High Road, Woodford New Road, Forest Rise, Whipps Cross, Lea Bridge Road and existing route. *(This possibly ran unnumbered).*
09.04.1909	1	Daily	Extended on Sundays from Cricklewood (Crown) to operate from Hendon (Upper Welsh Harp) via Edgware Road.
09.04.1909	10	Daily	Extended on Sundays from Leytonstone (Green Man) to South Woodford (George) via Hollybush Hill, Woodford Road.
09.04.1909	17	Daily	Extended on Sundays from Plaistow (Abbey Arms) to Rippleside (Ship & Shovel) via Barking Road, London Road, Ripple Road.
19.04.1909	5	Daily	Withdrawn daily between Chalk Farm (Adelaide) and Chalk Farm Road/Ferdinand Street and re-routed to operate from Hampstead Heath (South End Green) via Fleet Road, Southampton Road, Malden Road, Malden Crescent, Ferdinand Street.
25.04.1909	23	Sundays	New Route: Somerset House - Hampton Court (Vrow Walk) via Strand, Trafalgar Square (south side), Cockspur Street, Haymarket(?), Piccadilly Circus, Regent Street, Oxford Street, Marble Arch, Bayswater Road, High Street Notting Hill Gate*, Holland Park Avenue, Goldhawk Road*, Chiswick High Road, Kew Bridge, Kew Road, The Quadrant, George Street, Hill Street, Richmond Bridge, Richmond Road, York Street, King Street, Cross Deep, Waldegrave Road, Shacklegate Road*, Church Road, The Causeway, Park Road, Chestnut Avenue, Hampton Court Road.
06.05.1909	13	Daily	New Route: Peckham (Rye Lane) - Harringay (Queen's Head) via Peckham High Street, Peckham Road, Church Street*, Camberwell Green, Camberwell Road, Walworth Road*, Elephant & Castle, London Road, Westminster Bridge Road, Westminster Bridge, Bridge Street, Parliament Street, Whitehall, Cockspur Street, Pall Mall, Waterloo Place, Lower Regent Street, Piccadilly Circus, Regent Street, Mortimer Street (return via Margaret Street), Great Portland Street, Euston Road, Hampstead Road, Camden Town High Street*, Camden Road, Parkhurst Road, Seven Sisters Road, Green Lanes. *Joint operation with Tilling - see under that heading also.*
10.05.1909	3	Daily	Extended on weekdays from South Croydon (Swan & Sugar Loaf) to operate from South Croydon (Red Deer) via Brighton Road.
17.05.1909	22	Daily	New Route: Clapton (Lea Bridge Station) - Elephant & Castle via Lea Bridge Road, Lower Clapton Road, Mare Street, Graham Road, Dalston Lane, Kingsland Road, Shoreditch High Street, Norton Folgate, Bishopsgate Street*, Gracechurch Street, *[some journeys possibly ran via Threadneedle Street, Bank, King William Street]*, London Bridge, Borough High Street, Newington Causeway.

20.05.1909	4	Daily	Extended daily from Shepherds Bush (Bush Hotel) to operate from Wormwood Scrubs via Wood Lane.
20.05.1909	7	Daily	Extended daily from Wormwood Scrubs to operate from Shepherds Bush (Bush Hotel) via Wood Lane.
20.05.1909	15	Daily	Extended daily from Shepherds Bush (Bush Hotel) to operate from Wormwood Scrubs via Wood Lane.
10.06.1909	9	Daily	Extended weekdays from Leyton (Bakers' Arms) to Snaresbrook (Eagle) via Lea Bridge Road, Whipps Cross, Forest Rise, Snaresbrook Road.
10.06.1909	20	Daily	Extended daily from Tulse Hill (Tulse Hill Hotel) to West Norwood (Rosendale) via Norwood Road, Robson Road.
24.07.1909	9	Daily	Last day of operation between Whipps Cross and Snaresbrook (Eagle).
24.07.1909	25	Weekdays	New Route: Barnes (Avondale Road) - Piccadilly Circus via Mortlake High Street, Barnes Terrace*, Barnes High Street, Church Road, Castelnau, Hammersmith Bridge, Hammersmith Bridge Road, Hammersmith Broadway, Hammersmith Road, Kensington Road*, Kensington High Street, Kensington Road, Kensington Gore, Knightsbridge, Hyde Park Corner, Piccadilly. (see 9, 11)
25.07.1909	5	Daily	Last day of operation between Elephant & Castle and Camberwell Green.
25.07.1909	9	Daily	Last day of operation between Turnham Green Church and Hammersmith Broadway.
25.07.1909	11	Daily	Last day of operation between Barnes (Avondale Road) and Hammersmith Broadway (see 9, 25)
25.07.1909	15	Daily	Last day of operation. (see 17)
25.07.1909	18	Daily	Last day of operation apart from the Sunday service from Buckhurst Hill (Bald Faced Stag) – Bethnal Green. (see 8, 22)
26.07.1909	1	Daily	Extended daily from Elephant & Castle to Tower Bridge Road (Bricklayers' Arms) via New Kent Road.
26.07.1909	8	Daily	Withdrawn between Shepherds Bush (Bush Hotel) and Marble Arch and re-routed daily to operate from West Kilburn (Falcon) via Malvern Road*, Shirland Road, Formosa Street, Warwick Avenue, Clifton Gardens, Maida Vale, Edgware Road to Marble Arch and line of route. (see 18)
26.07.1909	9	Daily	Some journeys extended daily from Hammersmith Broadway to operate from Barnes (Avondale Road) via Barnes Terrace*, Barnes High Street, Church Road, Castelnau, Hammersmith Bridge, Hammersmith Bridge Road. (see 11, 25)
26.07.1909	12	Daily	Withdrawn between Bank and Ilford Broadway and re-routed daily to operate to Liverpool Street Station via Princes Street, Moorgate Street*, London Wall, Blomfield Street, Liverpool Street (return via New Broad Street*, Old Broad Street, Threadneedle Street). (covered by 8).
26.07.1909	17	Daily	Extended weekdays from Plaistow (Abbey Arms) to East Ham (Duke's Head) via Barking Road. (see 15)
26.07.1909	22	Daily	Extended daily from Clapton (Lea Bridge Station) to operate from Leyton (Bakers' Arms) and further extended on Sundays to operate from Epping Forest (Warren Wood House) *(referred to as 'Chingford' on contemporary listings)* via Epping New Road, Woodford High Road, Woodford New Road, Forest Rise, Whipps Cross, Lea Bridge Road.

26.07.1909	**24**	Daily	New Route: North Finchley (Swan & Pyramids) - Ebury Bridge (Monster) via High Road North Finchley, Ballards Lane, Regents Park Road, Finchley Road, Wellington Road, Park Road, Upper Baker Street*, York Place*, Baker Street, Portman Square (east side), Orchard Street, Oxford Street, Marble Arch, Park Lane, Hamilton Place, Hyde Park Corner, Grosvenor Place, Grosvenor Gardens (north side), Victoria Street, Wilton Road, Warwick Street*.
01.08.1909	**3**	Daily	Additional Service introduced on Sundays from Whyteleafe (Tavern) – South Croydon (Red Deer) via Purley Road, Godstone Road, Brighton Road.
01.08.1909	**9**	Daily	Extended on Sundays from Shoreditch Church to Snaresbrook (Eagle) via weekday route to Whipps Cross then via Forest Rise, Snaresbrook Road.

(b)   Other Operators

(i)   Amalgamated Omnibus Company Ltd.

05.06.1909		Daily	New Route: Cricklewood - Waterloo Station via Cricklewood Broadway, Shoot-Up Hill, Kilburn High Road, Maida Vale, Edgware Road, Chapel Street, Marylebone Road*, Euston Road, Tottenham Court Road, Charing Cross Road, St. Martins Place, Duncannon Street, Strand, Lancaster Place, Waterloo Bridge. (NOTE: Similar previous route by this operator ran via Marble Arch, Oxford Circus and Piccadilly Circus - see 29.10.1908 in Volume 1)
26.06.1909		Daily(?)	New Route: Liverpool Street Station - Victoria Station via New Broad Street*, Old Broad Street, Threadneedle Street (return Princes Street, Moorgate Street*, London Wall, Blomfield Street, Liverpool Street), Bank, Queen Victoria Street, Cannon Street, St. Paul's Churchyard, Ludgate Hill, Fleet Street, Strand, Charing Cross, Whitehall, Parliament Street, Parliament Square, Broad Sanctuary, Victoria Street.

(ii)   General Motor Cab Company

04.02.1909		Daily	Last press report of operation of the Portland Place - Earls Court route.

(iii)   Great Eastern London Motor Omnibus Company Ltd.

09.04.1909		Daily	Leyton (Bakers' Arms) - Marble Arch route re-extended on Sundays to operate from Epping Forest (Rising Sun) via Woodford New Road, Forest Rise, Whipps Cross, Lea Bridge Road.
06.05.1909		Daily	New Route: Epping Forest (Rising Sun) (Sundays) or Leyton (Bakers' Arms) (Weekdays) - Putney Station via Woodford New Road, Forest Rise, Whipps Cross, Lea Bridge Road, Lower Clapton Road, Mare Street, Cambridge Road*, Bethnal Green Road, Shoreditch High Street, Norton Folgate, Bishopsgate Street*, Threadneedle Street, Bank, Cheapside, Newgate Street, Holborn Viaduct, Holborn, High Holborn, New Oxford Street, Charing Cross Road, Shaftesbury Avenue, Piccadilly Circus, Piccadilly, Hyde Park Corner, Knightsbridge, Sloane Street, Sloane Square, Kings Road, Harwood Road, The Broadway Walham Green*, Fulham Road, Fulham High Street, Putney Bridge, Putney High Street.
28.05.1909		Daily	Last day of operation of the Stratford Broadway - Elephant & Castle route.
26.07.1909		Daily	New Route: West Kilburn (Falcon) - Victoria Station via Malvern Road*, Shirland Road, Formosa Street, Warwick Avenue, Clifton Gardens, Maida Vale, Edgware Road, Marble Arch, Park Lane, Hamilton Place, Hyde Park Corner, Grosvenor Place, Grosvenor Gardens (north side).

(iv)   London Central Omnibus Company Ltd.

11.04.1909 (?)   Sundays   New Route: Waterloo Station - Hampton Court (Vrow Walk) via Waterloo Bridge, Lancaster Place, Strand, Trafalgar Square, Piccadilly, Hyde Park Corner, Knightsbridge, Kensington Gore, Kensington Road, Kensington High Street, Hammersmith Road, Hammersmith Broadway, King Street, Chiswick High Road, Kew Bridge, Kew Road, George Street, Hill Street Richmond, (Petersham Road, Ham Common, Ham Road, Richmond Road, Kingston, Kingston Bridge, Hampton Court Road ?) *[This route possibly ran via Twickenham and Teddington rather than Kingston]*

(v)   London Electrobus Company Ltd.

08.02.1909   Daily   Victoria Station - Liverpool Street route extended daily from Victoria to operate from Earls Court via Cromwell Road, Brompton Road, Sloane Street, Sloane Square, Lower Sloane Street, Pimlico Road, Ebury Street.

15.02.1909   Daily   Earls Court - Liverpool Street route extended daily from Earls Court to operate from Fulham (Clarence) via Earls Court Road.

(vi) F.Newman

06.02.1909   Daily   Peckham (Rye Lane) - Oxford Circus route reported as withdrawn. *There is later photographic evidence that this service may have been resumed later. In addition 'Commercial Motor' of 27.03.1913 reports Newman as running two buses from Bromley to Farnborough at Easter 1913 and C.E.Lee noted that Newman's motors were withdrawn c.August 1914. In view of the uncertainty F.Newman's service has not been included in subsequent pages of this volume.*

(vii) Thomas Tilling Ltd.

06.05.1909   **13**   Daily   Peckham (Rye Lane) - Oxford Circus extended daily to Harringay (Queen's Head), numbered 13 and operated as a joint service with L.G.O.C. (q.v.).

06.05.1909   **21**   Daily   Sidcup (Black Horse) - Oxford Circus numbered 21 under an agreement signed on this date under which Tilling's motor services in London were operated by agreement with the L.G.O.C. and given route numbers.

MOTOR OMNIBUS ROUTES AS AT MONDAY 2ND AUGUST 1909

(i)   L.G.O.C.

1   Weekdays   Cricklewood (Crown) - Tower Bridge Road (Bricklayers' Arms)
        Sundays   Hendon (Upper Welsh Harp) - Tower Bridge Road (Bricklayers' Arms)

2   Daily   Ebury Bridge (Monster) - Childs Hill (Castle)

3   Weekdays   Oxford Circus - South Croydon (Red Deer)
        Sundays   South Croydon (Red Deer) – Whyteleafe (Tavern)

4   Daily   Wormwood Scrubs - Herne Hill (Half Moon Hotel)

5   Daily   Hampstead Heath (South End Green) - Elephant & Castle

6   Weekdays   Kensal Rise Station - Shoreditch Church
        Sundays   Kensal Rise Station - Charing Cross (Trafalgar Square)

7   Daily   Shepherds Bush (Bush Hotel) - Liverpool Street Station

8   Daily   West Kilburn (Falcon) - Seven Kings (Seven Kings Hotel)

9	Weekdays	Hammersmith Broadway - Whipps Cross
	Weekday Journeys	Barnes (Avondale Road) - Whipps Cross
	Sundays	Hammersmith - Snaresbrook (Eagle)
	Sunday Journeys	Barnes (Avondale Road) - Snaresbrook (Eagle)
10	Weekdays	Elephant & Castle - Leytonstone (Green Man)
	Sundays	Elephant & Castle - South Woodford (George)
11	Daily	Liverpool Street Station - Hammersmith Broadway
12	Daily	Turnham Green Church - Liverpool Street Station
13	Daily	Peckham (Rye Lane) - Harringay (Queen's Head) *Joint service with Tilling.*
14	Daily	Putney Station - Stratford Broadway
15		*Number not in use*
16	Daily	Victoria Station - Cricklewood (Crown)
17	Weekdays	Ealing Broadway (Railway Hotel) - East Ham (Duke's Head)
	Sundays	Ealing Broadway (Railway Hotel) - Rippleside (Ship & Shovel)
18	Sundays	Buckhurst Hill (Bald Faced Stag) - Bethnal Green (Green Man)
19	Daily	Clapham Junction (Northcote) - Highbury Barn (Tavern)
20	Daily	Hammersmith Broadway - West Norwood (Rosendale)
21		*See Tilling services*
22	Weekdays	Leyton (Bakers' Arms) - Elephant & Castle
	Sundays	Epping Forest (Warren Wood House) - Elephant & Castle
23	Sundays	Somerset House - Hampton Court (Vrow Walk) via Kew, Richmond, Teddington
24	Daily	North Finchley (Swan & Pyramids) - Ebury Bridge (Monster)
25	Weekdays	Barnes (Avondale Road) - Piccadilly Circus

(b)   Other Operators

      (i)   <u>Amalgamated Omnibus Company</u>

Daily	Cricklewood - Waterloo Station
Daily (?)	Liverpool Street Station - Victoria Station

      (ii)   <u>Great Eastern London Motor Omnibus Company Ltd.</u>

Daily	West Kilburn (Falcon) - Ilford Broadway
Daily	West Kilburn (Falcon) - Victoria Station
Weekdays	Leyton (Bakers' Arms) - Elephant & Castle
Sundays	Epping Forest (Rising Sun) - Elephant & Castle
Weekdays	Leyton (Bakers' Arms) - Oxford Circus
Sundays	Epping Forest (Rising Sun) - Marble Arch
Weekdays	Upton Park - Charing Cross
Sundays	Upton Park - Marble Arch

Weekdays Leyton (Bakers' Arms) - Putney Station
Sundays Epping Forest (Rising Sun) - Putney Station

(iii) <u>London and North Western Railway Company</u>

Weekdays Watford Junction Station - Croxley Green (Yorke Road)
Weekdays Watford Junction Station - Harrow & Wealdstone Station

Weekdays Harrow & Wealdstone Station – Harrow (Post Office)

(iv) <u>London Central Omnibus Company Ltd.</u>

Daily Chalk Farm (Adelaide) - Camberwell Green

Sundays Waterloo Station - Hampton Court

(v) <u>London Electrobus Company Ltd.</u>

Daily Fulham (Clarence) - Liverpool Street Station

(vi) <u>Metropolitan Steam Omnibus Company Ltd.</u>

Daily Barnes (Red Lion) - Piccadilly Circus

(vii) <u>Thomas Tilling Ltd.</u>

13 Daily Peckham (Rye Lane) - Harringay (Queen's Head) *Joint service with L.G.O.C.*

21 Daily Sidcup (Black Horse) - Oxford Circus

Daily Catford (Rushey Green) - Peckham (Rye Lane)

ALTERATIONS FROM 3RD AUGUST 1909 TO 28TH FEBRUARY 1910

NOTE: No record of the services operated on Christmas Day or Boxing Day, 25/26.12.1909 has been seen.

29.08.1909	**5**	Daily	Last day of operation between Waterloo Station and Elephant & Castle.
30.08.1909	**15**	Daily	New Route: Putney Station - Plaistow (Abbey Arms) via Putney High Street, Putney Bridge, Fulham High Street, Fulham Road, The Broadway Walham Green*, Fulham Road, Sydney Place, Onslow Square, Thurloe Place, Brompton Road, Knightsbridge, Hyde Park Corner, Piccadilly, Piccadilly Circus, Haymarket, Cockspur Street, Trafalgar Square (south side), Strand, Fleet Street, Ludgate Hill, St. Paul's Churchyard, Cannon Street, Queen Victoria Street, Bank, Cornhill, Leadenhall Street, Aldgate, Aldgate High Street, Whitechapel High Street, Commercial Road East*, East India Dock Road, Barking Road.
12.09.1909	**3**	Daily	Last day of operation between Whyteleafe (Tavern) and South Croydon (Red Deer).
15.09.1909	**3**	Daily	Last day of operation between South Croydon (Red Deer) and Streatham Common (Pied Bull).
15.09.1909	**13**	Daily	Last day of operation. *[Joint service with Thomas Tilling, q.v.]*
16.09.1909	**3**	Daily	Extended daily from Oxford Circus to Camden Town Station (Und.) via Mortimer Street (return via Margaret Street), Great Portland Street, Albany Street, Park Street*. *[Ticket proofs show a further extension to Harringay (Queens Head) to replace Route 13 was planned for 27.09.1909 but this never materialised].*

03.10.1909	**1**	Daily	Last day of operation between Hendon (Upper Welsh Harp) and Cricklewood (L.G.O.C. Garage).
10.10.1909	**1**	Daily	Extended on Mondays to Saturdays from Cricklewood (Crown) to operate from Cricklewood (L.G.O.C. Garage) as on Sundays.
10.10.1909	**10**	Daily	Last day of operation between South Woodford (George) and Leytonstone (Green Man).
10.10.1909	**17**	Daily	Last day of operation between East Ham (Duke's Head) and Rippleside (Ship and Shovel).
10.10.1909(?)	**18**	Sundays	Last day of operation.
10.10.1909(?)	**23**	Sundays	Last day of operation.
16.10.1909	**4**	Daily	Last day of operation between Wormwood Scrubs and Shepherds Bush (Bush Hotel).
16.10.1909	**7**	Daily	Last day of operation between Shepherds Bush (Bush Hotel) and Wormwood Scrubs.
28.10.1909	**22**	Daily	Extended Mondays to Saturdays from Leyton (Bakers' Arms) to operate from Whipps Cross via Lea Bridge Road (see 9). Also extended daily from Elephant & Castle to Brixton (George Canning)† via Newington Butts*, Kennington Park Road, Brixton Road, Effra Road. †*[Contemporary publicity referred to 'Tulse Hill, George Canning'].*
03.11.1909	**5**	Daily	Last day of operation between Hampstead Heath (South End Green) and Chalk Farm.
03.11.1909	**25**	Daily	Last day of operation. (See 9)
04.11.1909	**5**	Daily	Re-extended daily from Waterloo Station to Elephant & Castle.
04.11.1909	**9**	Daily	Withdrawn between Bank and Whipps Cross (weekdays) or Snaresbrook (Sundays) and re-routed daily to operate to Liverpool Street Station via Princes Street, Moorgate Street*, London Wall, Blomfield Street, Liverpool Street (return via New Broad Street*, Old Broad Street, Threadneedle Street) (see 22). Also entire service to operate daily from Barnes (Avondale Road) via Mortlake High Street instead of just journeys from Barnes (Avondale Road)(see 25).
05.12.1909	**4**	Daily	Last day of operation.
05.12.1909	**5**	Daily	Last day of operation. *[Withdrawn by agreement with London Central Omnibus Company, q.v.]*
05.12.1909	**10**	Daily	Last day of operation between Leytonstone (Green Man) and Stratford Broadway. (See 14)
06.12.1909	**14**	Daily	Extended daily from Stratford Broadway to operate from Leytonstone (Green Man) via Leytonstone High Road, Leytonstone Road, Maryland Point, The Grove. (See 10) Also withdrawn between Putney Bridge and Putney Station and re-routed daily to operate to Putney Common (Cricketers) via Lower Richmond Road.
02.01.1910	**22**	Daily	Last day of operation between Epping Forest (Warren Wood House) (Sundays) and Whipps Cross (Mondays to Saturdays) and Clapton (Lea Bridge Station).
12.01.1910	**24**	Daily	Last day of operation. *[M.E.T. trams commenced North Finchley to Childs Hill on 17.12.1909].*

13.01.1910	4	Daily	New Route: College Park (Masons' Arms) - Charing Cross via Harrow Road, Lord Hills Bridge, Porchester Road, Bishops Road*, Eastbourne Terrace, Praed Street, Edgware Road, Marble Arch, Oxford Street, Regent Street, Piccadilly Circus, Haymarket(?), Pall Mall East, Trafalgar Square. *[This replaced horse bus route 39 - M.E.T. trams commenced Harlesden to Paddington on 06.12.1909].*
13.01.1910	17	Daily	Extended daily from East Ham (Duke's Head) to Barking (Westbury) via Barking Road, London Road, Ripple Road.
09.02.1910	17	Daily	Last day of operation between East Ham (Duke's Head) and Barking (Westbury).

(b)   Other Operators

(i)   Great Eastern London Motor Omnibus Company Ltd.

09.09.1909	Weekdays	Leyton (Bakers' Arms) - Elephant & Castle route re-routed Mondays to Saturdays between Hackney and Shoreditch to operate via Graham Road, Dalston Lane, Kingsland Road to Shoreditch High Street and line of route.
12.09.1909	Sundays	Epping Forest (Rising Sun) - Elephant & Castle route re-routed on Sundays between Hackney and Shoreditch to operate via Graham Road, Dalston Lane, Kingsland Road to Shoreditch High Street and line of route. Also extended on Sundays from Epping Forest (Rising Sun) to operate from Epping Forest (Warren Wood House) via Epping New Road, Woodford New Road.
.10.1909	Weekdays	Upton Park - Charing Cross route withdrawn *[exact date not confirmed]*
.10.1909	Sundays	Upton Park - Marble Arch route withdrawn *[exact date not confirmed]*
.10.1909	Sundays	Epping Forest (Rising Sun) - Marble Arch route withdrawn between Epping Forest (Rising Sun) and Leyton (Bakers' Arms). *[exact date not confirmed]*

(ii)   London and North Western Railway Company

06.12.1909	Weekdays	Watford Junction Station - Croxley Green (Yorke Road) route extended Mondays to Saturdays from Watford Junction to operate from North Watford (Callowlands, Buckingham Road) via St. Albans Road, Station Road.

(iii)   London Central Omnibus Company

10.10.1909 (?)	Sundays	Waterloo Station - Hampton Court route withdrawn.

(iv)   London Electrobus Company

? date	Daily	The date when the extension to Fulham (Clarence) was finally withdrawn has not been confirmed. The basic service from Victoria Station to Liverpool Street Station was still operating in this period but with difficulty.

(v)   National Steam Car Company

02.11.1909	Daily	New Route: Shepherds Bush (White Horse) - Westminster Bridge Road (Christ Church) via Uxbridge Road, Holland Park Avenue, High Street Notting Hill Gate*, Bayswater Road, Marble Arch, Oxford Street, Regent Street, Piccadilly Circus, Lower Regent Street, Waterloo Place, Pall Mall, Cockspur Street, Whitehall, Parliament Street, Bridge Street, Westminster Bridge, Westminster Bridge Road.

.12.1909	Daily	Shepherds Bush (White Horse) - Westminster Bridge Road (Christ Church) route extended daily from Westminster Bridge Road to Elephant & Castle via Westminster Bridge Road, St. George's Road.

(vi) Thomas Tilling Ltd.

15.09.1909 **13**	Daily	Last day of operation. *[Joint route with L.G.O.C.]*
16.09.1909	Daily	Unnumbered Route re-instated: Peckham (Rye Lane) - Oxford Circus via former route 13.

MOTOR OMNIBUS ROUTES AS AT MONDAY 28TH FEBRUARY 1910

(i) L.G.O.C.

1	Daily	Cricklewood (L.G.O.C. Garage) - Tower Bridge Road (Bricklayers' Arms)
2	Daily	Ebury Bridge (Monster) - Childs Hill (Castle)
3	Daily	Streatham Common (Pied Bull) - Camden Town Station (Und.)
4	Daily	College Park (Masons' Arms) - Charing Cross (Trafalgar Square)
5		*Number not in use*
6	Weekdays	Kensal Rise Station - Shoreditch Church
	Sundays	Kensal Rise Station - Charing Cross (Trafalgar Square)
7	Daily	Wormwood Scrubs - Liverpool Street Station
8	Daily	West Kilburn (Falcon) - Seven Kings (Seven Kings Hotel)
9	Daily	Barnes (Avondale Road) - Liverpool Street Station
10	Daily	Stratford Broadway - Elephant & Castle
11	Daily	Hammersmith Broadway - Liverpool Street Station
12	Daily	Turnham Green Church - Liverpool Street Station
13		*Number not in use*
14	Daily	Leytonstone (Green Man) - Putney Common (Cricketers)
15	Daily	Putney Station - Plaistow (Abbey Arms)
16	Daily	Victoria Station - Cricklewood (Crown)
17	Daily	Ealing Broadway (Railway Hotel) - East Ham (Duke's Head)
18		*Number not in use*
19	Daily	Clapham Junction (Northcote) - Highbury Barn (Tavern)
20	Daily	Hammersmith Broadway - West Norwood (Rosendale)
21		*See Tilling services*
22	Daily	Clapton (Lea Bridge Station) - Brixton (George Canning)

(b) Other Operators

    (i)   Amalgamated Omnibus Company

Daily   Cricklewood - Waterloo Station

Daily   Liverpool Street Station - Victoria Station

    (ii)   Great Eastern London Motor Omnibus Company Ltd.

Daily   West Kilburn (Falcon) - Ilford Broadway
Daily   West Kilburn (Falcon) - Victoria Station

Weekdays Leyton (Bakers' Arms) - Elephant & Castle
Sundays Epping Forest (Warren Wood House) - Elephant & Castle

Weekdays Leyton (Bakers' Arms) - Oxford Circus
Sundays Leyton (Bakers' Arms) - Marble Arch

Weekdays Leyton (Bakers' Arms) - Putney Station
Sundays Epping Forest (Rising Sun) - Putney Station

    (iii)   London and North Western Railway Company

Weekdays North Watford (Callowlands) - Croxley Green (Yorke Road)

Weekdays Watford Junction Station - Harrow & Wealdstone Station

Weekdays Harrow & Wealdstone Station – Harrow (Post Office)

    (iv)   London Central Omnibus Company Ltd.

Daily   Chalk Farm (Adelaide) - Camberwell Green

    (v)   London Electrobus Company Ltd.

Daily   Victoria Station - Liverpool Street Station

    (vi)   Metropolitan Steam Omnibus Company Ltd.

Daily   Barnes (Red Lion) - Piccadilly Circus

    (vii)   National Steam Car Company

Daily   Shepherds Bush (White Horse) - Elephant & Castle

    (viii)   Thomas Tilling Ltd.

21   Daily   Sidcup (Black Horse) - Oxford Circus

Daily   Peckham (Rye Lane) - Oxford Circus

Daily   Catford (Rushey Green) - Peckham (Rye Lane)

ALTERATIONS FROM 1ST MARCH 1910 TO 31ST JULY 1910

NOTE: Public holidays during this period on which Sunday services usually operated were 25.03.1910 (Good Friday), 28.03.1910 (Easter Monday) and 16.05.1910 (Whit Monday).

(a)   L.G.O.C.

03.03.1910 **3** Daily Withdrawn between Streatham Common (Pied Bull) and Brixton (Lambeth Town Hall) and re-routed to operate from Brixton (George Canning) via Effra Road. *[To compete with Metropolitan Steam route].*

25.03.1910 **1** Daily Re-extended on Sundays from Cricklewood (L.G.O.C. Garage) to operate from Hendon (Upper Welsh Harp) via Edgware Road.

25.03.1910 **3** Daily Extended during the Easter Weekend only from Camden Town Statiion (Und.) to Hampstead Heath (South End Green) via Chalk Farm Road, Ferdinand Street, Malden Crescent, Malden Road, Southampton Road, Fleet Road.

25.03.1910 **4** Daily Extended on Sundays from College Park (Masons' Arms) to operate from Stonebridge Park (Coach & Horses) via Harrow Road*, Craven Park, Craven Park Road, High Street Harlesden, Harrow Road.

25.03.1910 **10** Daily Extended on Sundays from Stratford Broadway to operate from Buckhurst Hill (Bald Faced Stag) via Buckhurst Hill High Road, Woodford New Road, Woodford Road, Hollybush Hill, Leytonstone High Road, Leytonstone Road, Maryland Point, The Grove.

25.03.1910 **14** Daily Extended on Sundays from Leytonstone (Green Man) to operate from Wanstead (George) via Cambridge Park*. Also withdrawn between Putney Bridge and Putney Common (Cricketers) and re-routed daily to Putney Station via Putney High Street.

25.03.1910 **17** Daily Re-extended on Sundays from East Ham (Duke's Head) to Rippleside (Ship & Shovel) via Barking Road, London Road, Ripple Road.

25.03.1910 **18** Sundays New Route:
Somerset House - Hampton Court (Vrow Walk) via Strand, Trafalgar Square (south side), Cockspur Street, Haymarket(?), Piccadilly Circus, Piccadilly, Hyde Park Corner, Knightsbridge, Kensington Gore, Kensington Road, Kensington High Street, Kensington Road*, Hammersmith Road, Hammersmith Broadway, King Street, Chiswick High Road, Kew Bridge, Kew Road, The Quadrant, George Street, Hill Street, Richmond Bridge, Richmond Road, York Street, King Street, Cross Deep, Waldegrave Road, Shacklegate Road*, Church Road, The Causeway, Park Road, Chestnut Avenue, Hampton Court Road.

25.03.1910 **22** Daily Re-extended on Sundays from Clapton (Lea Bridge Station) to operate from Epping Forest (Warren Wood House) via Epping New Road, Woodford New Road, Forest Rise, Whipps Cross, Lea Bridge Road.

25.03.1910 **23** Sundays New Route: Somerset House – Hampton Court (Vrow Walk) via Strand, Trafalgar Square (south side), Cockspur Street, Haymarket(?), Piccadilly Circus, Piccadilly, Hyde Park Corner, Knightsbridge, Brompton Road, Thurloe Place, Onslow Square, Sydney Place, Fulham Road, The Broadway Walham Green*, Fulham Road, Fulham High Street, Putney Bridge, Putney High Street, Upper Richmond Road, Sheen Road, George Street, Hill Street, Lower Road, Petersham Road, Ham Common, Richmond Road*, Clarence Street, Kingston Bridge, Hampton Court Road.

30.03.1910 **22** Daily Last day of operation between Elephant & Castle and Brixton (George Canning).

04.04.1910 **5** Daily New Route: Barnsbury (Pocock Arms) – Putney Station extended on Sundays to Wimbledon (Rose & Crown) via Caledonian Road, Euston Road, Tottenham Court Road, Charing Cross Road, Shaftesbury Avenue, Piccadilly Circus, Piccadilly, Hyde Park Corner, Knightsbridge,

			Brompton Road, Thurloe Place, Onslow Square, Sydney Place, Fulham Road, The Broadway Walham Green*, Fulham Road, Fulham High Street, Putney Bridge, Putney High Street, Putney Hill, Putney Heath (east side)*, Parkside.
10.04.1910	**12**	Daily	Extended on Sundays from Turnham Green Church to operate from Kew Gardens via Kew Bridge, Chiswick High Road.
14.04.1910	**14**	Daily	Extended on Mondays to Saturdays from Leytonstone (Green Man) to operate from Wanstead (George) as on Sundays.
05.05.1910	**15**	Daily	Withdrawn between Putney Station and Putney Bridge and re-routed daily to operate from Putney Common (Cricketers) via Lower Richmond Road.
05.05.1910	**24**	Daily	New Route: Hampstead Heath (South End Green) – Victoria Station via Fleet Road, Southampton Road, Malden Road, Malden Crescent, Ferdinand Road, Chalk Farm Road, Camden Town High Street*, Hampstead Road, Tottenham Court Road, Charing Cross Road, St. Martins Place, Trafalgar Square (east side), Whitehall, Parliament Street, Parliament Square, Broad Sanctuary, Victoria Street.
11.05.1910	**22**	Daily	Last day of operation on Mondays to Saturdays between Clapton (Lea Bridge Station) and Dalston Junction.
12.05.1910			*Middle Row garage (D) opened.*
14.05.1910	**7**	Daily	Re-extended daily after 11.30 from Wormwood Scrubs to operate from Shepherds Bush via Wood Lane.
14.05.1910	**11**	Daily	Re-extended daily after 11.30 from Hammersmith Broadway to operate from Wormwood Scrubs via Wood Lane, The Lawn*, Shepherds Bush Road, Brook Green Road*.
08.06.1910	**17**	Daily	Last day of operation on Mondays to Saturdays between Plaistow (Abbey Arms) and East Ham (Duke's Head). (see 15)
09.06.1910	**15**	Daily	Extended daily from Plaistow (Abbey Arms) to East Ham (Duke's Head) via Barking Road. (see 17)
By 19.06.1910	**12**	Daily	Extended on Sundays from Kew Gardens to operate from Richmond via Kew Road. Also withdrawn on Sundays between Bank and Liverpool Street Station and re-routed on Sundays to operate to Shoreditch Church via Threadneedle Street, Bishopsgate Street*, Norton Folgate, Shoreditch High Street.
21.07.1910	**12**	Daily	Withdrawn on Mondays to Saturdays between Bank and Liverpool Street Station and re-routed on Mondays to Saturdays to operate to London Bridge Station via King William Street, London Bridge.
21.07.1910	**22**	Daily	Re-extended on Mondays to Saturdays from Dalston Junction to operate from Hackney Station via Graham Road, Dalston Lane.
24.07.1910	**9**	Daily	Last day of operation on Sundays between Piccadilly Circus and Liverpool Street Station.

(b)   Other Operators

(i)   Amalgamated Omnibus Company Ltd.

01.04.1910			*Operations taken over by British Automobile Development Ltd., subsidiary of British Electric Traction. (Used fleet name 'British').*
01.04.1910		Daily	Liverpool Street Station – Victoria Station route taken over by 'British'.

| 01.04.1910 | Daily | Cricklewood – Waterloo Station route not recorded as operating at this date, precise last day of operation not confirmed. |

| 05.04.1910 | | *'Amalgamated Omnibus Company' in liquidation.* |

(ii) <u>Great Eastern London Motor Omnibus Company Ltd.</u>

| 25.03.1910 (?) | Weekdays | Leyton (Bakers' Arms) – Putney Station route withdrawn on Mondays to Saturdays between Leyton (Bakers' Arms) and Bethnal Green. |

| 25.03.1910 (?) | Daily | West Kilburn (Falcon) – Victoria Station route extended daily from Victoria Station to Charing Cross (Trafalgar Square) via Victoria Street, Broad Sanctuary, Parliament Square, Parliament Street, Whitehall. |

| 25.03.1910 | Sundays | Leyton (Bakers' Arms) – Marble Arch route re-extended on Sundays from Leyton (Bakers' Arms) to operate from Epping Forest (Rising Sun) via Woodford New Road, Forest Rise, Whipps Cross, Lea Bridge Road. |

| 06.04.1910 | Weekdays | Bethnal Green – Putney Station route re-extended from Bethnal Green to operate from Hackney Station via Mare Street, Cambridge Road*. |

| 10.04.1910 | Daily | West Kilburn (Falcon) – Charing Cross (Trafalgar Square) route withdrawn on Sundays between Parliament Square and Trafalgar Square and re-routed on Sundays to operate to Elephant & Castle via Bridge Street, Westminster Bridge, Westminster Bridge Road, St. George's Road. |

| 07.05.1910 | Weekdays | Last day of operation of the West Kilburn (Falcon) – Charing Cross (Trafalgar Square) route on Mondays to Saturdays between Victoria Station and Charing Cross (Trafalgar Square). |

| 08.05.1910 | Sundays | Last day of operation of the West Kilburn (Falcon) – Elephant & Castle route on Sundays between Victoria Station and Elephant & Castle. |

(iii) <u>London Central Omnibus Company</u>

| 25.03.1910 | Sundays | <u>Route Re-instated</u>: Waterloo Station - Hampton Court (Vrow Walk) via Waterloo Bridge, Lancaster Place, Strand, Trafalgar Square, Piccadilly, Hyde Park Corner, Knightsbridge, Kensington Gore, Kensington Road, Kensington High Street, Hammersmith Road, Hammersmith Broadway, King Street, Chiswick High Road, Kew Bridge, Kew Road, George Street, Hill Street Richmond, (Petersham Road, Ham Common, Ham Road, Richmond Road, Kingston, Kingston Bridge, Hampton Court Road ?) *[This route possibly ran via Twickenham and Teddington rather than Kingston]* |

(iv) <u>London Electrobus Company</u>

| .03.1910 | Daily | Victoria Station – Liverpool Street Station route withdrawn. |

| 20.04.1910 | | *Press reports for this date report company 'no longer on the road'.* |

(v) <u>National Steam Car Company</u>

| 13.05.1910 | Daily | Shepherds Bush (White Horse) – Elephant & Castle route extended daily from Elephant & Castle to Peckham (Rye Lane) via Walworth Road*, Camberwell Road, Camberwell Green, Church Street*, Peckham Road, Peckham High Street. |

(vi) <u>Park Langley Estate</u>

| .07.1910 | Daily (?) | <u>New Route</u>: *(Contract service for residents only operated by General Motor Cab Company Ltd., who had operated 'Pullman' buses between Earls Court and Portland Place in 1908).* Beckenham Junction Station – |

Park Langley Estate (Whitecroft Way) via Beckenham High Street, Manor Road, Wickham Road, Wickham Way, Styles Way.

(vii)   Thomas Tilling Ltd.

20.03.1910 **13**	Daily	New Route: (incorporating unnumbered Peckham (Rye Lane) – Oxford Circus and Catford (Rushey Green) – Peckham routes). Bromley (Market Place) – Oxford Circus via London Road, Bromley Hill, Bromley Road*, Rushey Green, Lewisham High Street, Loampit Vale, Loampit Hill, Lewisham High Road*, New Cross Road, Queens Road, Peckham High Street, Peckham Road, Church Street*, Camberwell Green, Camberwell Road, Walworth Road*, Elephant & Castle, St. George's Road, Westminster Bridge Road, Westminster Bridge, Bridge Street, Parliament Street, Whitehall, Cockspur Street, Pall Mall, Waterloo Place, Lower Regent Street, Piccadilly Circus, Regent Street.	

MOTOR OMNIBUS ROUTES AS AT SUNDAY 31ST JULY 1910

(i)   L.G.O.C.

1   Weekdays   Cricklewood (L.G.O.C. Garage) – Tower Bridge Road (Bricklayers' Arms)
Sundays   Hendon (Upper Welsh Harp) – Tower Bridge Road (Bricklayers' Arms)

2   Daily   Ebury Bridge (Monster) - Childs Hill (Castle)

3   Daily   Brixton (George Canning) – Camden Town Station (Und.)

4   Weekdays   College Park (Masons' Arms) – Charing Cross (Trafalgar Square)
Sundays   Stonebridge Park (Coach & Horses) – Charing Cross (Trafalgar Square)

5   Weekdays   Barnsbury (Pocock Arms) – Putney Station
Sundays   Barnsbury (Pocock Arms) – Wimbledon (Rose & Crown)

6   Weekdays   Kensal Rise Station – Shoreditch Church
Sundays   Kensal Rise Station – Charing Cross (Trafalgar Square)

7   Daily (before 11.30)   Wormwood Scrubs – Liverpool Street Station
Daily (after 11.30)   Shepherds Bush – Liverpool Street Station

8   Daily   West Kilburn (Falcon) – Seven Kings (Seven Kings Hotel)

9   Weekdays   Barnes (Avondale Road) – Liverpool Street Station
Sundays   Barnes (Avondale Road) – Piccadilly Circus

10   Weekdays   Stratford Broadway – Elephant & Castle
Sundays   Buckhurst Hill (Bald Faced Stag) – Elephant & Castle

11   Daily (before 11.30)   Hammersmith Broadway – Liverpool Street Station
Daily (after 11.30)   Wormwood Scrubs – Liverpool Street Station

12   Weekdays   Turnham Green Church – London Bridge Station
Sundays   Richmond – Shoreditch Church

13   *See Tilling services*

14   Daily   Wanstead (George) – Putney Station

15   Daily   Putney Common (Cricketers) – East Ham (Duke's Head)

16   Daily   Victoria Station - Cricklewood (Crown)

17   Weekdays   Ealing Broadway (Railway Hotel) – Plaistow (Abbey Arms)
Sundays   Ealing Broadway (Railway Hotel) – Rippleside (Ship & Shovel)

| 18 | Sundays | Somerset House – Hampton Court (Vrow Walk) via Kew, Richmond and Teddington |

18   Sundays   Somerset House – Hampton Court (Vrow Walk) via Kew, Richmond and Teddington

19   Daily   Clapham Junction (Northcote) - Highbury Barn (Tavern)

20   Daily   Hammersmith Broadway – West Norwood (Rosendale)

21   *See Tilling services*

22   Weekdays   Hackney Station – Elephant & Castle
      Sundays   Epping Forest (Warren Wood House) – Elephant & Castle

23   Sundays   Somerset House – Hampton Court (Vrow Walk) via Putney, Richmond and Kingston

24   Daily   Hampstead Heath (South End Green) – Victoria Station

(b)   Other Operators

     (i)   British Automobile Development Ltd. ('British')

     Daily   Liverpool Street Station – Victoria Station

     (ii)   Great Eastern London Motor Omnibus Company Ltd.

     Daily   West Kilburn (Falcon) – Ilford Broadway

     Daily   West Kilburn (Falcon) – Victoria Station

     Weekdays   Leyton (Bakers' Arms) – Elephant & Castle
     Sundays   Epping Forest (Warren Wood House) – Elephant & Castle

     Weekdays   Leyton (Bakers' Arms) – Oxford Circus
     Sundays   Epping Forest (Rising Sun) – Marble Arch

     Weekdays   Hackney Station – Putney Station
     Sundays   Epping Forest (Rising Sun) – Putney Station

     (iii)   London and North Western Railway Company

     Weekdays   North Watford (Callowlands, Buckingham Road) – Croxley Green (Yorke Road)

     Weekdays   Watford Junction Station – Harrow & Wealdstone Station

     Weekdays   Harrow & Wealdstone Station – Harrow (Post Office)

     (iv)   London Central Omnibus Company Ltd.

     Daily   Chalk Farm (Adelaide) – Camberwell Green

     Sundays   Waterloo Station – Hampton Court (Vrow Walk)

     (v)   Metropolitan Steam Omnibus Company Ltd.

     Daily   Barnes (Red Lion) – Piccadilly Circus

     (vi)   National Steam Car Company

     Daily   Shepherds Bush (White Horse) – Peckham (Rye Lane)

(vii)   Park Langley Estate

Daily (?)   Beckenham Junction Station – Park Langley Estate (Whitecroft Way) *(estate residents only)*
Operated by General Motor Cab Company Ltd.

(viii) Thomas Tilling Ltd.

13   Daily   Bromley (Market Place) – Oxford Circus

21   Daily   Sidcup (Black Horse) – Oxford Circus

ALTERATIONS FROM 1ST AUGUST 1910 TO 31ST DECEMBER 1910

NOTE: Public holidays during this period on which Sunday services usually operated were 01.08.1910 (August Bank Holiday Monday). No record of services operated on 25/26.12.1910 (Christmas Day and Boxing Day has been seen.

04.08.1910   **4**   Daily   Extended Mondays to Saturdays from College Park (Masons' Arms) to operate from Harlesden (Crown) via High Street Harlesden, Harrow Road.

01.09.1910   **4**   Daily   Extended daily from Charing Cross to Waterloo Station via Strand, Wellington Street*, Waterloo Bridge.

01.09.1910   **8**   Daily   Withdrawn daily between West Kilburn (Falcon) and Maida Vale and re-routed to operate from Willesden Green (Spotted Dog) via Willesden Lane, Kilburn High Road to Maida Vale and line of route.

29.10.1910   **7**   Daily   Last day of operation between Shepherds Bush and Wormwood Scrubs.

29.10.1910   **11**   Daily   Last day of operation between Wormwood Scrubs and Shepherds Bush (The Lawn).

30.10.1910   **5**   Daily   Last day of operation on Sundays between Putney Station and Wimbledon (Rose & Crown).

30.10.1910   **18**   Sundays   Last day of operation. (Re-introduced 14.04.1911 as Route 52).

30.10.1910   **23**   Sundays   Last day of operation. (Re-introduced 14.04.1911 as Route 51).

31.10.1910   *Clay Hall garage (P) opened.*

31.10.1910   **25**   Daily   New Route: Victoria Station – Old Ford (Lady Franklin) via Wilton Road, Victoria Street (return via Buckingham Palace Road), Grosvenor Gardens (north side), Grosvenor Place, Hyde Park Corner, Piccadilly, Old Bond Street, New Bond Street, Oxford Street, New Oxford Street, High Holborn, Holborn, Holborn Viaduct, Newgate Street, Cheapside, Bank, Threadneedle Street, Bishopsgate Street*, Norton Folgate, Shoreditch High Street, Bethnal Green Road, Green Street*, Roman Road, St. Stephen's Road, Old Ford Road.

14.11.1910   **4**   Daily   Extended daily from Waterloo Station to Elephant & Castle via Waterloo Road, London Road.

12.12.1910 **13**	Daily		<u>New Route</u>: London Bridge Station - Childs Hill (Castle) via London Bridge, King William Street, Cannon Street, St. Paul's Churchyard, Ludgate Hill, Fleet Street, Strand, Trafalgar Square (south side), Cockspur Street, Haymarket, Piccadilly Circus, Regent Street, Oxford Street, Orchard Street, Portman Square (east side), Baker Street, York Place*, Upper Baker Street*, Park Road, Wellington Road, Finchley Road.
14.12.1910 **15**	Daily		Last day of operation between Plaistow (Abbey Arms) and East Ham (Duke's Head). (see 17).
15.12.1910 **17**	Daily		Extended Mondays to Saturdays from Plaistow (Abbey Arms) to East Ham (Duke's Head) via Barking Road. (see 15)
.12.1910 (?)**10**	Daily		Withdrawn on Sundays between Buckhurst Hill (Bald Faced Stag) and Stratford Broadway. *[Shown in L.G.O.C. printed list for December 1910 but not in January 1911 – actual last date of operation not confirmed].*
.12.1910 (?)**22**	Daily		Withdrawn on Sundays between Epping Forest (Warren Wood House) and Hackney Station. *[Shown in L.G.O.C. printed list for December 1910 but not in January 1911 – actual last date of operation not confirmed].*

(b)   <u>Other Operators</u>

   (i)   <u>Great Eastern London Motor Omnibus Company Ltd.</u>

30.10.1910 (?)	Sundays	Last day of operation of the Epping Forest (Rising Sun) – Marble Arch route on Sundays between Epping Forest (Rising Sun) and Leyton (Bakers' Arms).
.12.1910 (?)	Sundays	Last day of operation of the Epping Forest (Rising Sun) – Putney Station route on Sundays between Epping Forest (Rising Sun) and Hackney Station.

   (ii)   <u>London Central Omnibus Company Ltd.</u>

30.10.1910 (?)	Sundays	Last day of operation of the Waterloo Station – Hampton Court (Vrow Walk) route.

   (iii)   <u>Metropolitan Steam Omnibus Company Ltd.</u>

30.09.1910	Daily	Last day of operation of the Barnes (Red Lion) – Piccadilly Circus route.
01.10.1910	Daily	<u>New Route</u>: Piccadilly Circus – Piccadilly Circus via Haymarket(?), Cockspur Street, Whitehall, Parliament Street, Parliament Square, Broad Sanctuary, Victoria Street, Grosvenor Gardens (north side), Grosvenor Place, Hyde Park Corner, Piccadilly. *(circular route in this direction only)*.
15.10.1910	Daily	<u>New Route</u>: Earls Court – Kings Cross Station via Cromwell Road, Brompton Road, Knightsbridge, Hyde Park Corner, Piccadilly, Piccadilly Circus, Regent Street, Oxford Street, Tottenham Court Road, Euston Road.
26.10.1910	Daily	Last day of operation of the Piccadilly Circus circular route.
26.10.1910	Daily	Last day of operation of the Earls Court – Kings Cross route between Oxford Circus and Kings Cross.
27.10.1910	Daily	<u>New Route</u>: Hammersmith Broadway – Piccadilly Circus via Hammersmith Broadway, Hammersmith Road, Kensington Road*, Kensington High Street, Kensington Road, Kensington Gore, Knightsbridge, Hyde Park Corner, Piccadilly.

| 02.11.1910 | | Daily | Hammersmith Broadway – Piccadilly Circus route extended daily from Hammersmith Broadway to operate from Fulham (Salisbury) via Dawes Road, The Broadway Walham Green*, Dawes Road, Crown Road*, Fulham Palace Road, Queen Street*. |

(v)   Thomas Tilling Ltd.

10.12.1910	**13**	Daily	Last day of operation on Mondays to Saturdays. Sunday service continued but ran as an unnumbered route.
10.12.1910	**21**	Daily	Last day of operation on Mondays to Saturdays. Sunday service continued but ran as an unnumbered route.
12.12.1910		Daily	Unnumbered Route Re-instated daily: Peckham (Rye Lane) – Oxford Circus via Peckham High Street, Peckham Road, Church Street*, Camberwell Green, Camberwell Road, Walworth Road*, Elephant & Castle, St. George's Road, Westminster Bridge Road, Westminster Bridge, Bridge Street, Parliament Street, Whitehall, Cockspur Street, Pall Mall, Waterloo Place, Lower Regent Street, Piccadilly Circus, Regent Street.
12.12.1910		Weekdays	New Unnumbered Monday to Saturday Route: Sidcup (Black Horse) – Lewisham via Foots Cray Road, Eltham High Street, Eltham Hill, Eltham Green, Eltham Road, Lee High Road, Lee Bridge, Lewisham High Street.
12.12.1910		Weekdays	New Unnumbered Monday to Saturday Route: Bromley (Market Place) – Lewisham via London Road, Bromley Hill, Bromley Road*, Rushey Green, Lewisham High Street.

MOTOR OMNIBUS ROUTES AS AT SATURDAY 31ST DECEMBER 1910

(a)   L.G.O.C.

1 Weekdays Cricklewood (L.G.O.C. Garage) – Tower Bridge Road (Bricklayers' Arms)
       Sundays   Hendon (Upper Welsh Harp) – Tower Bridge Road (Bricklayers' Arms)

2 Daily   Ebury Bridge (Monster) - Childs Hill (Castle)

3 Daily   Brixton (George Canning) – Camden Town Station (Und.)

4 Weekdays Harlesden (Crown) – Elephant & Castle
       Sundays   Stonebridge Park (Coach & Horses) – Elephant & Castle

5 Daily   Barnsbury (Pocock Arms) – Putney Station

6 Weekdays Kensal Rise Station – Shoreditch Church
       Sundays   Kensal Rise Station – Charing Cross (Trafalgar Square)

7 Daily   Wormwood Scrubs – Liverpool Street Station

8 Daily   Willesden Green (Spotted Dog) – Seven Kings (Seven Kings Hotel)

9 Weekdays Barnes (Avondale Road) – Liverpool Street Station
       Sundays   Barnes (Avondale Road) – Piccadilly Circus

10 Daily   Stratford Broadway – Elephant & Castle

11 Daily   Shepherds Bush (The Lawn) – Liverpool Street Station

12 Weekdays Turnham Green Church – London Bridge Station
       Sundays   Richmond – Shoreditch Church

| 13 | Daily | London Bridge Station - Childs Hill (Castle) |

13   Daily   London Bridge Station - Childs Hill (Castle)

14   Daily   Wanstead (George) – Putney Station

15   Daily   Putney Common (Cricketers) – Plaistow (Abbey Arms)

16   Daily   Victoria Station - Cricklewood (Crown)

17   Weekdays   Ealing Broadway (Railway Hotel) – East Ham (Duke's Head)
      Sundays   Ealing Broadway (Railway Hotel) – Rippleside (Ship & Shovel)

18   *Number not in use*

19   Daily   Clapham Junction (Northcote) - Highbury Barn (Tavern)

20   Daily   Hammersmith Broadway – West Norwood (Rosendale)

21   *Number not in use*

22   Daily   Hackney Station – Elephant & Castle

23   *Number not in use*

24   Daily   Hampstead Heath (South End Green) – Victoria Station

25   Daily   Victoria Station – Old Ford (Lady Franklin)

(b)   Other Operators

       (i)   British Automobile Development Ltd. ('British')

       Daily   Liverpool Street Station – Victoria Station

       (ii)   Great Eastern London Motor Omnibus Company Ltd.

       Daily   West Kilburn (Falcon) – Ilford Broadway

       Daily   West Kilburn (Falcon) – Victoria Station

       Weekdays   Leyton (Bakers' Arms) – Elephant & Castle
       Sundays   Epping Forest (Warren Wood House) – Elephant & Castle

       Weekdays   Leyton (Bakers' Arms) – Oxford Circus
       Sundays   Leyton (Bakers' Arms) – Marble Arch

       Daily   Hackney Station – Putney Station

       (iii) London and North Western Railway Company

       Weekdays   North Watford (Callowlands, Buckingham Road) – Croxley Green (Yorke Road)

       Weekdays   Watford Junction Station – Harrow & Wealdstone Station

       Weekdays   Harrow & Wealdstone Station – Harrow (Post Office)

       (iv)   London Central Omnibus Company Ltd.

       Daily   Chalk Farm (Adelaide) – Camberwell Green

       (v)   Metropolitan Steam Omnibus Company Ltd.

       Daily   Earls Court – Oxford Circus

Daily   Fulham (Salisbury) – Piccadilly Circus

(vi) National Steam Car Company

Daily   Shepherds Bush (White Horse) – Peckham (Rye Lane)

(vi) Park Langley Estate

Daily (?)   Beckenham Junction Station – Park Langley Estate (Whitecroft Way) *(estate residents only)*
Operated by General Motor Cab Company Ltd.

(viii) Thomas Tilling Ltd.

Weekdays Bromley (Market Place) – Lewisham
Sundays   Bromley (Market Place) – Oxford Circus

Weekdays Sidcup (Black Horse) – Lewisham
Sundays   Sidcup (Black Horse) – Oxford Circus

Daily   Peckham (Rye Lane) – Oxford Circus

ALTERATIONS FROM 1ST JANUARY 1911 TO 7TH AUGUST 1911

NOTE: Public holidays during this period on which Sunday services usually operated were 14.04.1911 (Good Friday), 17.04.1911 (Easter Monday), 05.06.1911 (Whit Monday) and 07.08.1911 (August Bank Holiday Monday).

(a)   L.G.O.C.

09.01.1911	**33**	Weekdays 10.00-17.00	New Route: Oxford Circus – Zoological Gardens via Regent Street, Mortimer Street (return via Margaret Street, Great Portland Street, Albany Street, Albert Road*).
01.02.1911	**4**	Daily	Last day of operation. (See 18)
02.02.1911	**18**	Daily	New Route: Kensal Green (Masons' Arms) – Camberwell Green, extended on Sundays to operate from Stonebridge Park (Coach & Horses) via Harrow Road*, Craven Park, Craven Park Road, High Street Harlesden, Harrow Road, Edgware Road, Chapel Street, Marylebone Road*, Euston Road, Grays Inn Road, Holborn, St. Andrew's Street, Shoe Lane, St. Bride Street, Farringdon Street, Ludgate Circus, New Bridge Street, Blackfriars Bridge, Blackfriars Road, London Road, Elephant & Castle, Walworth Road*, Camberwell Road. (See 4) *NOTE: Terminus at Kensal Green previously described as 'College Park'.*
.03.1911			*Turnham Green garage (C) opened.*
26.03.1911	**13**	Daily	Last day of operation on Sundays between London Bridge Station and Charing Cross (Trafalgar Square).
30.03.1911	**13**	Daily	Extended daily from Childs Hill (Castle) to Hendon (Bell) via Finchley Road, Golders Green Road, Brent Street.
01.04.1911			*L.G.O.C. acquired the Great Eastern London Motor Omnibus Company Ltd. and, under L.G.O.C. control, its routes were integrated with those of the L.G.O.C. or given route numbers during April 1911.*
01.04.1911			*Garages acquired from Great Eastern: Forest Gate, Green Street garage (Q)* *Kilburn, Lonsdale Road garage (G)* *Leyton, Lea Bridge Road garage (K)*

06.04.1911	**21**	Daily	New Route: Newington Green – Old Kent Road (Canal Bridge) via Mildmay Park, Southgate Road, Bridport Place*, Mintern Street, New North Road, East Road, City Road, Finsbury Pavement, Moorgate Street*, Princes Street, Bank, King William Street, London Bridge, Borough High Street, Great Dover Street, Old Kent Road.
06.04.1911	**22**	Daily	Withdrawn between Bank and Elephant & Castle and re-routed daily to operate to Putney Station via Cheapside, Newgate Street, Holborn Viaduct, Holborn, High Holborn, New Oxford Street, Charing Cross Road, Shaftesbury Avenue, Piccadilly Circus, Piccadilly, Hyde Park Corner, Knightsbridge, Sloane Street, Sloane Square, Kings Road, New Kings Road, Putney Bridge, Putney High Street. (Replaced former Great Eastern route although taking different route in Fulham. See also Route 36).
06.04.1911	**35**	Daily	New Route: Elephant & Castle – Leyton (Bakers' Arms) extended on Sundays to Epping Forest (Warren Wood House) via Newington Causeway, Borough High Street, London Bridge, King William Street, Gracechurch Street, Bishopsgate, Norton Folgate, Shoreditch High Street, Kingsland Road, Dalston Lane, Pembury Road, Cricketfield Road, Downs Road, Lower Clapton Road, Lea Bridge Road, Whipps Cross, Forest Rise, Woodford New Road, Epping New Road. (Former Great Eastern route numbered). *[NOTE:initial LGOC tickets and maps erroneously show this route operating via Bank rather then direct via Gracechurch Street].*
06.04.1911	**36**	Daily	New Route: West Kilburn (Falcon) – Liverpool Street Station via Malvern Road*, Walterton Road, Harrow Road, Lord Hills Bridge, Porchester Road, Bishops Road*, Eastbourne Terrace, Praed Street, Edgware Road, Marble Arch, Park Lane, Hamilton Place, Hyde Park Corner, Grosvenor Place, Grosvenor Gardens (north side), Victoria Street, Vauxhall Bridge Road, Vauxhall Bridge, Kennington Lane, Harleyford Road, Kennington Oval, Harleyford Street, Kennington Park Road, Newington Butts*, Elephant & Castle, Newington Causeway, Borough High Street, London Bridge, King William Street, Bank, Princes Street, Moorgate Street*, London Wall, Blomfield Street, Liverpool Street (return via New Broad Street*, Old Broad Street, Threadneedle Street). (Replacing former Great Eastern route between West Kilburn and Victoria but by slightly different route between West Kilburn and Edgware Road and Route 22 between Elephant & Castle and Bank)
06.04.1911	**37**	Daily	New Route: West Kilburn (Falcon) – Ilford Broadway via Malvern Road*, Shirland Road, Formosa Street, Warwick Avenue, Clifton Road, Edgware Road, Marble Arch, Oxford Street, New Oxford Street, High Holborn, Holborn, Holborn Viaduct, Newgate Street, Cheapside, Bank, Cornhill, Leadenhall Street, Aldgate, Aldgate High Street, Whitechapel High Street, Whitechapel Road, Mile End Road, Bow Road, Stratford High Street, Stratford Broadway, Romford Road, Ilford Hill. (Former Great Eastern route numbered).
09.04.1911	**54**	Sundays	New Route: Marble Arch – Leyton (Bakers' Arms) via Oxford Street, New Oxford Street, Hart Street*, Vernon Place, Theobalds Road, Rosebery Avenue, St. John Street, Islington High Street, Upper Street, Essex Road, Balls Pond Road, Dalston Lane, Graham Road, Mare Street, Lower Clapton Road, Lea Bridge Road. (Replaced former Great Eastern route but by different routeing between New Oxford Street and Hackney)
11.04.1911	**35**	Daily	Extended on Mondays to Saturdays from Leyton (Bakers' Arms) to Walthamstow (Hoe Street Station) via Hoe Street. *[This was a bifurcation from the Sunday operation].*
14.04.1911	**1**	Daily	Additional service introduced on Sundays if the weather is fine: Edgware (Royal Oak) – Charing Cross (Trafalgar Square) via Edgware Road* and line of route.

14.04.1911	**18**	Daily	Extended on Sundays from Camberwell Green to Tulse Hill (Tulse Hill Hotel) via Denmark Hill, Coldharbour Lane, Hinton Road, Milkwood Road, Norwood Road. Re-routed *[believed on same date]* between Holborn and Ludgate Circus via Charterhouse Street, Farringdon Street instead of via St. Andrew Street, Shoe Lane, St. Bride Street.
14.04.1911	**51**	Sundays	New Route: (Ran as 23 in 1910 – last day of operation 30.10.1910) Somerset House – Hampton Court (Vrow Walk) via Strand, Trafalgar Square (south side), Cockspur Street, Haymarket(?), Piccadilly Circus, Piccadilly, Hyde Park Corner, Knightsbridge, Brompton Road, Thurloe Place, Onslow Square, Sydney Place, Fulham Road, The Broadway Walham Green*, Fulham Road, Fulham High Street, Putney Bridge, Putney High Street, Upper Richmond Road, Sheen Road, George Street, Hill Street, Lower Road, Petersham Road, Ham Common, Richmond Road*, Clarence Street, Kingston Bridge, Hampton Court Road.
14.04.1911	**52**	Sundays	New Route: (Ran as 18 in 1910 – last day of operation 30.10.1910) Somerset House - Hampton Court (Vrow Walk) via Strand, Trafalgar Square (south side), Cockspur Street, Haymarket(?), Piccadilly Circus, Piccadilly, Hyde Park Corner, Knightsbridge, Kensington Gore, Kensington Road, Kensington High Street, Kensington Road*, Hammersmith Road, Hammersmith Broadway, King Street, Chiswick High Road, Kew Bridge, Kew Road, The Quadrant, George Street, Hill Street, Richmond Bridge, Richmond Road, York Street, King Street, Cross Deep, Waldegrave Road, Shacklegate Road*, Church Road, The Causeway, Park Road, Chestnut Avenue, Hampton Court Road.
14.04.1911	**53**	Sundays	New Route: (Ran as daily 24 in 1910 – last day of operation 12.01.1910) North Finchley (Swan & Pyramids) – Ebury Bridge (Monster) via High Road North Finchley, Ballards Lane, Regents Park Road, Finchley Road, Wellington Road, Park Road, Upper Baker Street*, York Place*, Baker Street, Portman Square (east side), Orchard Street, Oxford Street, Marble Arch, Park Lane, Hamilton Place, Hyde Park Corner, Grosvenor Place, Grosvenor Gardens (north side), Victoria Street, Wilton Road, Warwick Street*
14.04.1911	**54**	Sundays	Extended on Sundays from Leyton (Bakers' Arms) to Epping Forest (Rising Sun) via Lea Bridge Road, Whipps Cross, Forest Rise, Woodford New Road.
14.04.1911	**55**	Sundays	New Route: (Ran as an extension of 10 in 1910) Elephant & Castle – Buckhurst Hill (Bald Faced Stag) via Newington Causeway, Borough High Street, London Bridge, King William Street, Gracechurch Street, Fenchurch Street, Aldgate, Aldgate High Street, Whitechapel High Street, Whitechapel Road, Mile End Road, Bow Road, Stratford High Street, Stratford Broadway, The Grove, Maryland Point, Leytonstone Road, Leytonstone High Road, Hollybush Hill, Woodford Road, Woodford High Road, Buckhurst Hill High Road.
By 05.1911	**7**	Daily	Alternate buses re-routed between Ladbroke Grove and Westbourne Grove via Elgin Crescent, Kensington Park Road and Archer Street* instead of Cornwall Road*, Richmond Road*.
07.05.1911	**17**	Daily	Last day of operation on Sundays between East Ham (Duke's Head) and Rippleside (Ship & Shovel). (See 23)
08.05.1911	**4**	Daily	New Route: Islington (Angel) – Elephant & Castle via Goswell Road, Aldersgate Street, St. Martins-le-Grand, Cheapside, Bank, King William Street, London Bridge, Borough High Street, Newington Causeway.
08.05.1911	**5**	Daily	Extended daily from Barnsbury (Pocock Arms) to operate from Tollington Park (Stapleton Hall Tavern) via Stroud Green Road, Wells Terrace, Fonthill Road, Seven Sisters Road, Holloway Road, Camden Road, Caledonian Road and line of route. Also re-extended on Sundays

from Putney Station to Wimbledon (Rose & Crown) via Putney Hill, Putney Heath (east side)*, Parkside. *[NOTE: Maps up until July 1912 show the route running via the full length of Stroud Green Road to Seven Sisters Road but this was unlikely due to the low railway bridges. Tickets show Fonthill Road from the start and include Wells Terrace from June 1912]*

08.05.1911	12	Daily	Withdrawn on Mondays to Saturdays between Oxford Circus and London Bridge (see 17) and re-routed Mondays to Saturdays from Oxford Circus to operate to Peckham (Rye Lane) via Regent Street, Piccadilly Circus, Lower Regent Street, Waterloo Place, Pall Mall, Cockspur Street, Whitehall, Parliament Street, Bridge Street, Westminster Bridge, Westminster Bridge Road, St. George's Road, Elephant & Castle, Walworth Road*, Camberwell Road, Camberwell Green, Church Street*, Peckham Road, Peckham High Street. *Became joint service with Thomas Tilling Ltd. (q.v.) in competition with National Steam Car.*
08.05.1911	17	Daily	Withdrawn on Mondays to Saturdays between Bank and East Ham (Duke's Head) and re-routed Mondays to Saturdays from Bank to operate to London Bridge Station via King William Street, London Bridge. (See 12 and 23)
08.05.1911	23	Daily	New Route: Shepherds Bush (weekdays), Marble Arch (Sundays) – East Ham (Duke's Head) extended on Sundays to Rippleside (Ship & Shovel) via Uxbridge Road, Holland Park Avenue, High Street Notting Hill Gate*, Bayswater Road, Marble Arch, Oxford Street, New Oxford Street, High Holborn, Holborn, Holborn Viaduct, Newgate Street, Cheapside, Bank, Cornhill, Leadenhall Street, Aldgate, Aldgate High Street, Whitechapel High Street, Commercial Road East*, East India Dock Road, Barking Road, London Road, Ripple Road. (see 17)
08.05.1911	30	Weekdays	New Route: Kings Cross Station – Fulham Cross via Euston Road, Great Portland Street, Margaret Street (return via Mortimer Street), Regent Street, Piccadilly Circus, Piccadilly, Hyde Park Corner, Knightsbridge, Brompton Road, Cromwell Road, Earls Court Road, Richmond Road*, Lillie Road.
11.05.1911	10	Daily	Extended daily from Stratford Broadway to operate from Wanstead (George) via Cambridge Park*, Leytonstone High Road, Leytonstone Road, Maryland Point, The Grove and line of route. (See 14).
11.05.1911	14	Daily	Withdrawn daily between Wanstead (George) and Piccadilly Circus and re-routed daily to operate from Hornsey Rise (Favourite) via Hornsey Road, Seven Sisters Road, Holloway Road, Camden Road, Caledonian Road, Pentonville Road, Euston Road, Tottenham Court Road, Charing Cross Road, Shaftesbury Avenue to Piccadilly Circus and line of route. (See 10)
15.05.1911	4	Daily	Extended daily from Islington (Angel) to operate from Holloway (Nags Head) via Holloway Road, Liverpool Road, High Street Islington.
15.05.1911	21	Daily	Extended daily from Newington Green to operate from Finsbury Park (Manor House) via Green Lanes.
18.05.1911	7	Daily	Re-extended daily from Wormwood Scrubs to operate from Shepherds Bush via Wood Lane.
18.05.1911	11	Daily	Re-extended daily from Shepherds Bush to operate from Wormwood Scrubs via Wood Lane.
28.05.1911	23	Daily	Extended on Sundays from Shepherds Bush to operate from Ealing (Railway Hotel) via Ealing Broadway, The Mall, Uxbridge Road, Acton High Street, Acton Vale, Uxbridge Road and line of route.
28.05.1911	37	Daily	Last day of operation.

03.06.1911	**4**	Daily	Last day of operation. *[L.G.O.C. Map & Guide states 'temporarily suspended']*
04.06.1911(?)	**20**	Daily	Extended on Sundays from Hammersmith Broadway to operate from Putney Station via Putney High Street, Putney Bridge, Fulham High Street, Fulham Palace Road.
04.06.1911	**30**	Daily	Introduced on Sundays and extended daily from Fulham Cross to Putney Station and on Sundays to Petersham (Dysart Arms) via Lillie Road, Fulham Palace Road, Fulham High Street, Putney Bridge, Putney High Street, Upper Richmond Road, Sheen Road, George Street, Hill Street, Lower Road*.
05.06.1911	**18**	Daily	Withdrawn on Sundays between Loughborough Junction and Tulse Hill (Tulse Hill Hotel) and re-routed on Sundays and extended on Mondays to Saturdays from Camberwell Green to operate to Clapham Common (Plough) via Denmark Hill, Coldharbour Lane, Acre Lane, Clapham Park Road.
12.06.1911	**22**	Daily	Extended daily from Hackney Station to operate from Homerton (Clapton Park Tavern) via Chatsworth Road, Dunlace Road, Median Road, Lower Clapton Road, Mare Street and line of route.
06.07.1911			*Hackney garage (N) opened.*
06.07.1911	**27**	Daily	New Route: Turnham Green Church – Stoke Newington (Weavers Arms) via Chiswick High Road, King Street, Hammersmith Broadway, Hammersmith Road, Kensington Road*, Kensington High Street, Church Street*, High Street Notting Hill Gate*, Pembridge Villas, Westbourne Grove, Bishops Road*, Eastbourne Terrace, Praed Street, Chapel Street, Marylebone Road*, Euston Road, Pentonville Road, High Street Islington, Upper Street, Essex Road, Newington Green Road, Newington Green (west side), Albion Road, Church Street, Stoke Newington High Street.
07.07.1911	**18**	Daily	Re-routed daily between Coldharbour Lane and Acre Lane via Gresham Road, Brixton Road.
17.07.1911	**26**	Daily	New Route: West Kilburn (Falcon) – Hackney Wick via Malvern Road*, Shirland Road, Formosa Street, Warwick Avenue, Clifton Gardens, Maida Vale, Edgware Road, Marble Arch, Oxford Street, New Oxford Street, High Holborn, Holborn, Holborn Viaduct, Newgate Street, Cheapside, Bank, Threadneedle Street, Bishopsgate, Norton Folgate, Shoreditch High Street, Hackney Road, Cambridge Road*, Mare Street, Well Street, Cassland Road, Wick Road.
31.07.1911	**30**	Daily	Re-routed daily between Brompton Road and Richmond Road* via Thurloe Place, Old Brompton Road.
31.07.1911	**28**	Daily	New Route: Wandsworth Bridge (Wandsworth Bridge Tavern) – West Hampstead (West End Green) via Wandsworth Bridge Road, Harwood Road, The Broadway Walham Green*, North End Road, Lillie Road, Richmond Road*, Earls Court Road, Kensington Road*, Kensington High Street, Church Street*, High Street Notting Hill Gate*, Pembridge Villas, Richmond Road*, Cornwall Road*, Great Western Road, Walterton Road, Cambridge Road*, Kilburn High Road, Quex Road, West End Lane.
.08.1911	**5**	Daily	Tollington Park (Stapleton Hall Tavern) terminus re-designated Stroud Green (Stapleton Hall Tavern).

(b)   Other Operators

(i)   Great Eastern London Motor Omnibus Company Ltd.

Discussion between the L.G.O.C. and Great Eastern regarding a pooling arrangement had fallen through in 1909, but some conversations continued in 1910 whilst competition increased. L.G.O.C. then commenced a campaign to acquire Great Eastern shares and eventually an amalgamation was agreed, the Great Eastern shareholders receiving L.G.O.C. shares in payment. The Great Eastern shareholders approved the agreement on 06.03.1911. The date for accountancy purposes was 01.01.1911. On 02.05.1911 the L.G.O.C. Board decided to purchase the Great Eastern outright and wind it up. The fleet and services were under L.G.O.C. control from early April. Routes were allocated L.G.O.C. numbers.

.04.1911	Weekdays	Leyton (Bakers' Arms) – Oxford Circus route withdrawn.
02.04.1911	Sundays	Leyton (Bakers' Arms) – Marble Arch route. Last day of operation. (See L.G.O.C. Route 54 (which followed a different route via Islington)).
02.04.1911	Sundays	Epping Forest (Warren Wood House) – Elephant & Castle route. Last day of operation. (See L.G.O.C. Route 35).
05.04.1911	Weekdays	Leyton (Bakers' Arms) – Elephant & Castle route. Last day of operation. (See L.G.O.C. Route 35).
05.04.1911	Daily	West Kilburn (Falcon) – Ilford Broadway route. Last day of operation. (See L.G.O.C. Route 37).
05.04.1911	Daily	West Kilburn (Falcon) – Victoria Station route. Last day of operation. (See L.G.O.C. Route 36).
05.04.1911	Daily	Hackney Station – Putney Station route. Last day of operation. (See L.G.O.C. Route 22 (which followed a different route in Fulham)).

(ii)   London Central Omnibus Company Ltd.

14.04.1911	Sundays	Route Re-instated: Waterloo Station - Hampton Court (Vrow Walk) via Waterloo Bridge, Lancaster Place, Strand, Trafalgar Square, Piccadilly, Hyde Park Corner, Knightsbridge, Kensington Gore, Kensington Road, Kensington High Street, Hammersmith Road, Hammersmith Broadway, King Street, Chiswick High Road, Kew Bridge, Kew Road, George Street, Hill Street Richmond, (Petersham Road, Ham Common, Ham Road, Richmond Road, Kingston, Kingston Bridge, Hampton Court Road ?). *[This route possibly ran via Twickenham and Teddington rather than Kingston]*

(iii)   Metropolitan Steam Omnibus Company Ltd.

17.05.1911	Daily	Earls Court – Oxford Circus route extended daily from Oxford Circus to Camden Town Station (Und.) via Regent Street, Mortimer Street (return via Margaret Street), Great Portland Street, Albany Street, Park Street*.
18.05.1911		*A Board minute records that all vehicles were removed to Lots Road garage – opened 17.05.1911 (?).*
11.06.1911	Daily	Earls Court – Camden Town route extended on Sundays from Earls Court to operate from Richmond Bridge via Hill Street, George Street, Sheen Road, Upper Richmond Road, Putney High Street, Putney Bridge, Fulham High Street, Fulham Road, The Broadway Walham Green*, North End Road, Lillie Road, Richmond Road*, Earls Court Road to Cromwell Road and line of route.

09.07.1911	Sundays	Richmond Bridge – Camden Town route extended on Sundays from Richmond Bridge to operate from Petersham (Dysart Arms) via Petersham Road, Lower Road* to Hill Street and line of route.
24.07.1911	Daily	Fulham (Salisbury) – Piccadilly Circus route. Last day of operation.
25.07.1911	Weekdays	Earls Court – Camden Town route extended on Monday to Saturday from Earls Court to operate from Fulham (Salisbury) via Dawes Road, North End Road, Lillie Road, Richmond Road*, Earls Court Road to Cromwell Road and line of route.
25.07.1911	Weekdays	New Route: Fulham (Salisbury) – Brixton (Lambeth Town Hall) via Dawes Road, Fulham Road, Fulham High Street, Putney Bridge, Putney High Street, Upper Richmond Road, West Hill, Wandsworth High Street, East Hill, St. John's Hill, St. John's Road, Battersea Rise, Clapham Common North Side, Old Town, The Pavement, Clapham Park Road, Acre Lane.
30.07.1911	Sundays	New Route: Petersham (Dysart Arms) – Brixton (Lambeth Town Hall) via Petersham Road, Lower Road*, Hill Street, George Street, Sheen Road, Upper Richmond Road, West Hill, Wandsworth High Street, East Hill, St. John's Hill, St. John's Road, Battersea Rise, Clapham Common North Side, Old Town, The Pavement, Clapham Park Road, Acre Lane.

(iv) National Steam Car Company Ltd.

20.02.1911	Daily	Shepherds Bush (White Horse) – Peckham (Rye Lane) route extended daily from Peckham (Rye Lane) to Peckham Rye (King's Arms) via Rye Lane.
25.04.1911	Daily	New Route: Victoria Station – Liverpool Street Station via Victoria Street, Broad Sanctuary, Parliament Square, Parliament Street, Whitehall, Charing Cross, Strand, Fleet Street, Ludgate Hill, St. Paul's Churchyard, Cannon Street, Queen Victoria Street, Bank, Princes Street, Moorgate Street*, London Wall, Blomfield Street, Liverpool Street (return via New Broad Street*, Old Broad Street, Threadneedle Street).
16.04.1911	Sundays	New Route: *(in competition with Thomas Tilling Ltd.)* Sidcup (Black Horse) - Oxford Circus via Sidcup High Street, Foots Cray Road*, Victoria Road*, Eltham High Street, Eltham Hill, Eltham Green, Eltham Road, Lee High Road, Lee Bridge, Lewisham High Street, Loampit Vale, Loampit Hill, Lewisham High Road*, New Cross Road, Queens Road, Peckham High Street, Peckham Road, Church Street*, Camberwell Green, Camberwell Road, Walworth Road*, Elephant & Castle, St. George's Road, Westminster Bridge Road, Westminster Bridge, Bridge Street, Parliament Street, Whitehall, Cockspur Street, Pall Mall, Waterloo Place, Lower Regent Street, Piccadilly Circus, Regent Street.
30.05.1911	Weekdays	New Route: Shepherds Bush (Victoria Tavern) – Liverpool Street Station via Uxbridge Road, Holland Park Avenue, High Street Notting Hill Gate*, Bayswater Road, Marble Arch, Oxford Street, New Oxford Street, High Holborn, Holborn, Holborn Viaduct, Newgate Street, Cheapside, Bank, Princes Street, Moorgate Street*, London Wall, Blomfield Street, Liverpool Street (return via New Broad Street*, Old Broad Street, Threadneedle Street).

(v) Park Langley Estate

.06.1911	Daily (?)	Beckenham Junction Station – Park Langley Estate (Whitecroft Way) route. *Contract transferred to Commercial Cab Hirers Ltd.*

(vi)   Thomas Tilling Ltd.

08.05.1911 **12**   Weekdays   Peckham – Oxford Circus route became joint service with L.G.O.C. (q.v.) and extended weekdays from Oxford Circus to Turnham Green Church via Oxford Street, Marble Arch, Bayswater Road, High Street Notting Hill Gate*, Holland Park Avenue, Goldhawk Road*, Chiswick High Road. Adopted L.G.O.C. number 12.

MOTOR OMNIBUS ROUTES AS AT TUESDAY 8TH AUGUST 1911

(a)   L.G.O.C.

1   Weekdays   Cricklewood (L.G.O.C. Garage) – Tower Bridge Road (Bricklayers' Arms)
          Sundays   Hendon (Upper Welsh Harp) – Tower Bridge Road (Bricklayers' Arms)
          Sundays   Edgware (Royal Oak) – Charing Cross (Trafalgar Square) *Additional service only operated if fine.*

2   Daily   Ebury Bridge (Monster) - Childs Hill (Castle)

3   Daily   Brixton (George Canning) – Camden Town Station (Und.)

4   *Number not in use*

5   Weekdays   Stroud Green (Stapleton Hall Tavern) – Putney Station
          Sundays   Stroud Green (Stapleton Hall Tavern) – Wimbledon (Rose & Crown)

6   Weekdays   Kensal Rise Station – Shoreditch Church
          Sundays   Kensal Rise Station – Charing Cross (Trafalgar Square)

7   Daily   Shepherds Bush – Liverpool Street Station

8   Daily   Willesden Green (Spotted Dog) – Seven Kings (Seven Kings Hotel)

9   Weekdays   Barnes (Avondale Road) – Liverpool Street Station
          Sundays   Barnes (Avondale Road) – Piccadilly Circus

10   Daily   Wanstead (George) – Elephant & Castle

11   Daily   Wormwood Scrubs – Liverpool Street Station

12   Weekdays   Turnham Green Church – Peckham (Rye Lane)   *Joint with Thomas Tilling Ltd.*
          Sundays   Richmond – Shoreditch Church

13   Weekdays   London Bridge Station – Hendon (Bell)
          Sundays   Charing Cross (Trafalgar Square) – Hendon (Bell)

14   Daily   Hornsey Rise (Favourite) – Putney Station

15   Daily   Putney Common (Cricketers) – Plaistow (Abbey Arms)

16   Daily   Victoria Station - Cricklewood (Crown)

17   Weekdays   Ealing Broadway (Railway Hotel) – London Bridge Station
          Sundays   Ealing Broadway (Railway Hotel) – East Ham (Duke's Head)

18   Weekdays   Kensal Green (Masons' Arms) – Clapham Common (Plough)
          Sundays   Stonebridge Park (Coach & Horses) – Clapham Common (Plough)

19   Daily   Clapham Junction (Northcote) - Highbury Barn (Tavern)

20   Weekdays   Hammersmith Broadway – West Norwood (Rosendale)
          Sundays   Putney Station – West Norwood (Rosendale)

21   Daily   Finsbury Park (Manor House) – Old Kent Road (Canal Bridge)

22	Daily	Homerton (Clapton Park Tavern) – Putney Station
23	Weekdays Sundays	Shepherds Bush (Bush Hotel) – East Ham (Duke's Head) Ealing Broadway (Railway Hotel) – Rippleside (Ship & Shovel)
24	Daily	Hampstead Heath (South End Green) – Victoria Station
25	Daily	Victoria Station – Old Ford (Lady Franklin)
26	Daily	West Kilburn (Falcon) – Hackney Wick
27	Daily	Turnham Green Church – Stoke Newington (Weavers Arms)
28	Daily	Wandsworth Bridge (Tavern) – West Hampstead (West End Green)
29		*Number not in use*
30	Weekdays Sundays	Kings Cross Station – Putney Station Kings Cross Station – Petersham (Dysart Arms)
31 – 32		*Numbers not in use*
33	Weekdays 10.00 – 17.00	Oxford Circus – Zoological Gardens
34		*Number not in use*
35	Weekdays Sundays	Elephant & Castle – Walthamstow (Hoe Street Station) via Hoe Street Elephant & Castle – Epping Forest (Warren Wood House) via Whipps Cross
36	Daily	West Kilburn (Falcon) – Liverpool Street Station
37 – 50		*Numbers not in use*
51	Sundays	Somerset House – Hampton Court (Vrow Walk) via Putney, Richmond and Kingston
52	Sundays	Somerset House – Hampton Court (Vrow Walk) via Kew, Richmond and Teddington
53	Sundays	North Finchley (Swan & Pyramids) – Ebury Bridge (Monster)
54	Sundays	Marble Arch – Epping Forest (Rising Sun)
55	Sundays	Elephant & Castle – Buckhurst Hill (Bald Faced Stag)

(b) Other Operators

    (i) British Automobile Development Ltd. ('British')

Daily	Liverpool Street Station – Victoria Station

    (ii) London and North Western Railway Company

Weekdays	North Watford (Callowlands, Buckingham Road) – Croxley Green (Yorke Road)
Weekdays	Watford Junction Station – Harrow & Wealdstone Station
Weekdays	Harrow & Wealdstone Station – Harrow (Post Office)

    (iii) London Central Omnibus Company Ltd.

Daily	Chalk Farm (Adelaide) – Camberwell Green
Sundays	Waterloo Station – Hampton Court (Vrow Walk)

(iv) Metropolitan Steam Omnibus Company Ltd.

Weekdays Fulham (Salisbury) – Camden Town Station (Und.)
Sundays   Petersham (Dysart Arms) – Camden Town Station (Und.)

Weekdays Fulham (Salisbury) – Brixton (Lambeth Town Hall)

Sundays   Petersham (Dysart Arms) – Brixton (Lambeth Town Hall)

(v) National Steam Car Company

Daily   Shepherds Bush (White Horse) – Peckham Rye (King's Arms)

Daily   Victoria Station – Liverpool Street Station

Sundays   Sidcup (Black Horse) - Oxford Circus

Weekdays   Shepherds Bush (Victoria Tavern) – Liverpool Street Station

(vi) Park Langley Estate

Daily (?)   Beckenham Junction Station – Park Langley Estate (Whitecroft Way) *(residents only)*
            Operated by Commercial Cab Hirers Ltd.

(vii) Thomas Tilling Ltd.

12   Weekdays Peckham (Rye Lane) – Turnham Green (Church). *Joint service with L.G.O.C.*

Weekdays Bromley (Market Place) – Lewisham
Sundays   Bromley (Market Place) – Oxford Circus

Weekdays Sidcup (Black Horse) – Lewisham
Sundays   Sidcup (Black Horse) – Oxford Circus

ALTERATIONS FROM 9TH AUGUST 1911 TO 31ST DECEMBER 1911

(a)   L.G.O.C.

7.08.1911	**15**	Daily	Extended on Mondays to Saturdays from Plaistow (Abbey Arms) to East Ham (Duke's Head) via Barking Road.
.09.1911	**33**	Weekdays	Last day of operation.
.09.1911	**31**	Daily	New Route: Chelsea (Stanley Arms) – South Hampstead (North Star) via Edith Grove, Redcliffe Gardens, Earls Court Road, Kensington High Street, Church Street*, High Street Notting Hill Gate*, Pembridge Road, Pembridge Villas, Richmond Road*, Cornwall Road*, Great Western Road, Walterton Road, Cambridge Road*, Cambridge Avenue, Belsize Road.
01.10.1911	**12**	Daily	Last day of operation of the Sunday service between Richmond and Shoreditch (renumbered 57).
01.10.1911	**54**	Sundays	Last day of operation between Leyton (Baker's Arms) and Epping Forest (Rising Sun).
05.10.1911	**12**	Weekdays	Extended Mondays to Saturdays from Peckham (Rye Lane) to Peckham Rye (King's Arms) via Rye Lane. Introduced on Sundays Turnham Green Church to Peckham Rye (King's Arms) as on weekdays. *See also Thomas Tilling Ltd. below.*

08.10.1911	**57**	Sundays	Sunday Operation on Route 12 renumbered 57: Richmond (Queen's Head) – Shoreditch Church via The Quadrant, Kew Road, Kew Bridge, Chiswick High Road, Goldhawk Road*, Holland Park Avenue, High Street Notting Hill Gate*, Bayswater Road, Marble Arch, Oxford Street, New Oxford Street, High Holborn, Holborn, Holborn Viaduct, Newgate Street, Cheapside, Bank, Threadneedle Street, Bishopsgate, Norton Folgate, Shoreditch High Street.
08.10.1911	**22**	Daily	Last day of operation on Sundays.
08.10.1911	**52**	Sundays	Last day of operation. (Re-introduced 05.04.1912).
15.10.1911	**1**	Daily	Last day of operation of the additional Sunday service between Edgware (Royal Oak) and Charing Cross.
15.10.1911	**5**	Daily	Last day of operation on Sundays between Putney Station and Wimbledon (Rose & Crown).
15.10.1911	**9**	Daily	Extended on Sundays from Piccadilly Circus to Liverpool Street Station as on weekdays.
15.10.1911	**35**	Daily	Withdrawn on Sundays between Leyton (Baker's Arms) and Epping Forest (Warren Wood House) and re-routed on Sundays to operate to Walthamstow (Hoe Street Station) as on Mondays to Saturdays. (See 56).
15.10.1911	**56**	Sundays	Sunday Operation on Route 35 renumbered 56: Elephant & Castle – Epping Forest (Warren Wood House) via Newington Causeway, Borough High Street, London Bridge, King William Street, Gracechurch Street, Bishopsgate, Norton Folgate, Shoreditch High Street, Kingsland Road, Dalston Lane, Pembury Road, Cricketfield Road, Downs Road, Lower Clapton Road, Lea Bridge Road, Whipps Cross, Forest Rise, Woodford New Road, Epping New Road.
19.10.1911	**8**	Daily	Extended daily from Willesden Green (Spotted Dog) to operate from Willesden (White Hart) via Church Road, Willesden High Road.
22.10.1911	**7**	Daily	Last day of operation between Shepherds Bush and Wormwood Scrubs.
22.10.1911	**11**	Daily	Last day of operation between Wormwood Scrubs and Shepherds Bush.
23.10.1911	**21**	Daily	Extended daily from Finsbury Park (Manor House) to operate from Wood Green (Fishmongers' Arms) via Green Lanes, Jolly Butchers Hill, Wood Green High Road, Green Lanes and also extended daily from Old Kent Road (Canal Bridge) to Deptford Broadway via Old Kent Road, New Cross Road.
.11.1911			*Holloway garage (J) opened.*
02.11.1911			*Complete reallocation of garage code letters as follows:*

Acton	A became E		Holloway	? became J*	
Albany Street	L	" A	Kilburn	G " K	
Athol Street	S	" C	Leyton, Lea Bridge Road	K " T	
Battersea	T	" B	Middle Row	D " X	
Clay Hall	P	" Y	Mortlake	W " M	
Cricklewood	E	" W	Normand Road, Fulham	X " R	
Dalston	O	" D	Norwood	U " N	
Farm Lane, Fulham	Y	" F	Old Kent Road	V " P	
Felsham Road, Putney	Z	" Q	Shepherds Bush	B " S	
Forest Gate	Q	" G	Turnham Green	C " V	
Hackney	N	" H	Upton Park	R " U	
				*probably always J	

05.11.1911	**30**	Daily	Last day of operation on Sundays between Putney Station and Petersham (Dysart Arms).
12.11.1911	**7**	Daily	Last day of operation of journeys via Elgin Crescent, Archer Street*. (See 32).
13.11.1911	**32**	Daily	New Route: Charing Cross (Trafalgar Square) – Shepherds Bush via Cockspur Street, Haymarket(?), Piccadilly Circus, Regent Street, Oxford Street, Marble Arch, Edgware Road, Praed Street, Eastbourne Terrace, Bishops Road*, Westbourne Grove, Archer Street*, Elgin Crescent, Ladbroke Grove, Cambridge Gardens, St. Mark's Road, St. Quintin Avenue, North Pole Road, Scrubs Lane, Wood Lane.
19.11.1911	**21**	Daily	Last day of operation between Wood Green (Fishmongers' Arms) and Newington Green. (Replaced by 29 between Wood Green and Manor House but Green Lanes 'under repair', i.e. closed for tramway reconstruction).
20.11.1911	**29**	Daily	New Route: Victoria Station – Wood Green (Fishmongers' Arms) via Victoria Street, Broad Sanctuary, Parliament Square, Parliament Street, Whitehall, Trafalgar Square, St. Martins Place, Charing Cross Road, Tottenham Court Road, Hampstead Road, Camden Town High Street*, Camden Road, Parkhurst Road, Seven Sisters Road, Green Lanes, Wood Green High Road, Jolly Butchers Hill, Green Lanes.
By 12.1911	**27**	Daily	Extended daily from Stoke Newington (Weavers Arms) to Stoke Newington (Birdcage) via Stamford Hill.
07.12.1911	**23**	Daily	Extended Mondays to Saturdays from Shepherds Bush to operate from Acton Vale (King's Arms) via Uxbridge Road also from East Ham (Duke's Head) to Barking (Westbury) via Barking Road, London Road, Ripple Road.
07.12.1911	**27**	Daily	Extended Mondays to Saturdays from Turnham Green Church to operate from Richmond (Queen's Head) via George Street (return via Duke Street, Richmond Green, King Street), The Quadrant, Kew Road, Kew Bridge, Chiswick High Road to line of route.
07.12.1911	**31**	Daily	Extended daily from South Hampstead (North Star) to Finchley Road Station (Met) via Finchley Road.
17.12.1911	**23**	Daily	Extended on Sundays from Ealing Broadway (Railway Hotel) to operate from South Ealing (New Inn) via St. Mary's Road, Ealing Green, Ealing High Street to Ealing Broadway and line of route.
18.12.1911	**17**	Daily	Extended on Mondays to Saturdays from Ealing (Railway Hotel) to operate from South Ealing (New Inn) via St. Mary's Road, Ealing Green, Ealing High Street to Ealing Broadway and line of route.
19.12.1911(?)	**30**	Daily	Re-routed between Oxford Circus and Hyde Park Corner via Oxford Street, Marble Arch, Park Lane instead of Regent Street, Piccadilly Circus, Piccadilly.

(b)   Other Operators

(i)   London Central Omnibus Company Ltd.

08.10.1911	Sundays	Last day of operation of the Waterloo Station – Hampton Court route.
11.11.1911	Daily	New Route: Kingston (Market Place) – Thames Ditton (Angel) via St. James Road, Penrhyn Road, Surbiton Road, Maple Road, Balaclava Road, Effingham Road, Ewell Road, Thornhill Road, Portsmouth Road.

18.11.1911	Daily	Kingston (Market Place) – Thames Ditton (Angel) route re-routed daily between Maple Road and Balaclava Road via Claremont Road, Surbiton Station, Victoria Road, Brighton Road to Balaclava Road and line of route.
18.11.1911	Daily	New Route: Kingston (Market Place) – Thames Ditton (Fountain) via High Street, Portsmouth Road, St Leonards Road.
19(?).11.1911	Daily	Kingston (Market Place) – Thames Ditton (Angel) route extended on Sundays from Kingston to operate from Kew Bridge via Kew Road, The Quadrant, George Street, Hill Street, Richmond Bridge, Richmond Road, York Street, King Street, Cross Deep, Waldegrave Road, Teddington High Street, Ferry Road, Kingston Road, Upper Teddington Road, High Street Hampton Wick, Kingston Bridge, Thames Street.
09.12.1911	Daily	Kingston (Market Place) – Thames Ditton (Fountain) route withdrawn between Portsmouth Road and Thames Ditton (Fountain) and re-routed daily to operate to Esher (Bear) via Portsmouth Road, High Street Esher.
16.12.1911	Weekdays	Kingston (Market Place) – Thames Ditton (Angel) route extended on Mondays to Saturdays to operate from Richmond via Richmond Bridge, Richmond Road, York Street, King Street, Cross Deep, Waldegrave Road, Teddington High Street, Ferry Road, Kingston Road, Upper Teddington Road, High Street Hampton Wick, Kingston Bridge, Thames Street.

(ii)   Metropolitan Steam Omnibus Company Ltd.

07.09.1911	Weekdays	Fulham (Salisbury) – Camden Town Station (Und.) route withdrawn between Fulham (Salisbury) and Earls Court Station.
10.09.1911	Sundays	Petersham (Dysart Arms) – Camden Town Station (Und.) route withdrawn between Petersham (Dysart Arms) and Earls Court Station.
25.09.1911	Daily	New Route: Fulham (Salisbury) – Charing Cross (Trafalgar Square) extended Monday to Saturday to Liverpool Street Station via Dawes Road, Jerdan Place, The Broadway Walham Green*, Harwood Road, Kings Road, Sloane Square, Lower Sloane Street, Pimlico Road, Buckingham Palace Road, Victoria Street, Broad Sanctuary, Parliament Square, Parliament Street, Whitehall, Charing Cross, Strand, Fleet Street, Ludgate Hill, St. Paul's Churchyard, Cannon Street, Queen Victoria Street, Bank, Princes Street, Moorgate Street*, London Wall, Blomfield Street, Liverpool Street (return via New Broad Street*, Old Broad Street, Threadneedle Street).
08(?).10.1911	Sundays	Last day of operation of the Petersham (Dysart Arms) – Brixton (Lambeth Town Hall) route.
12.10.1911	Daily	Earls Court Station – Camden Town Station (Und.) route extended daily from Earls Court Station to operate from Chelsea (Lots Road) via Kings Road, Harwood Road, The Broadway Walham Green*, North End Road, Lillie Road, Richmond Road*, Earls Court Road.
15.10.1911	Weekdays	Fulham (Salisbury) – Brixton (Lambeth Town Hall) route introduced on Sundays as on Mondays to Saturdays.
25.11.1911	Weekdays	Last day of operation of the Fulham (Salisbury) – Liverpool Street Station route.
26.11.1911	Sundays	Last day of operation of the Fulham (Salisbury) – Charing Cross (Trafalgar Square) route.

| 27.11.1911 | Weekdays(?) | New Route: Chelsea (Lots Road) – Shoreditch Church via Kings Road, Harwood Road, The Broadway Walham Green*, Fulham Road, Fulham High Street, Putney Bridge, Putney High Street, Upper Richmond Road, West Hill, Wandsworth High Street, East Hill, St. John's Hill, St. John's Road, Battersea Rise, Clapham Common North Side, Old Town, The Pavement, Clapham Road, Kennington Park Road, Newington Butts*, Newington Causeway, Borough High Street, London Bridge, King William Street, Gracechurch Street, Bishopsgate, Norton Folgate, Shoreditch High Street. |

(iii) National Steam Car Company Ltd.

03.10.1911	Sundays	Last day of operation of the Sidcup (Black Horse) - Oxford Circus route.
03.11.1911	Daily	New Route: Cricklewood (Crown) – Peckham (Rye Lane) via Cricklewood Broadway, Shoot-up Hill, Kilburn High Road, Maida Vale, Edgware Road, Marble Arch, Park Lane, Hamilton Place, Hyde Park Corner, Grosvenor Place, Grosvenor Gardens (north side), Victoria Street, Vauxhall Bridge Road, Vauxhall Bridge, Bridgefoot, Kennington Lane, Harleyford Road, Kennington Oval, Harleyford Street, Camberwell New Road, Church Street*, Peckham Road, Peckham High Street.
29.11.1911	Daily	Last day of operation of the Cricklewood (Crown) – Peckham (Rye Lane) route.
30.11.1911	Daily	New Route: Liverpool Street Station – Peckham (Rye Lane) via New Broad Street*, Old Broad Street, Threadneedle Street (return via Princes Street, Moorgate Street*, London Wall, Blomfield Street, Liverpool Street), King William Street, London Bridge, Borough High Street, Newington Causeway, Elephant & Castle, Walworth Road*, Camberwell Road, Camberwell Green, Church Street*, Peckham Road, Peckham High Street.

(iv) Thomas Tilling Ltd.

| 05.10.1911 | 12 | Weekdays | Extended on Mondays to Saturdays from Peckham (Rye Lane) to operate from Peckham Rye (King's Arms) via Rye Lane. *Joint service with L.G.O.C.* |

MOTOR OMNIBUS ROUTES AS AT MONDAY 1ST JANUARY 1912

(a) L.G.O.C.

1	Weekdays	Cricklewood (L.G.O.C. Garage) – Tower Bridge Road (Bricklayers' Arms)
	Sundays	Hendon (Upper Welsh Harp) – Tower Bridge Road (Bricklayers' Arms)
2	Daily	Ebury Bridge (Monster) - Childs Hill (Castle)
3	Daily	Brixton (George Canning) – Camden Town Station (Und.)
4		*Number not in use*
5	Daily	Stroud Green (Stapleton Hall Tavern) – Putney Station
6	Weekdays	Kensal Rise Station – Shoreditch Church
	Sundays	Kensal Rise Station – Charing Cross (Trafalgar Square)
7	Daily	Wormwood Scrubs – Liverpool Street Station
8	Daily	Willesden (White Hart) – Seven Kings (Seven Kings Hotel)
9	Daily	Barnes (Avondale Road) – Liverpool Street Station

10   Daily   Wanstead (George) – Elephant & Castle

11   Daily   Shepherds Bush – Liverpool Street Station

12   Daily   Turnham Green Church – Peckham Rye (King's Arms)   *Joint with Thomas Tilling Ltd on weekdays.*

13   Weekdays   London Bridge Station - Hendon (Bell)
          Sundays   Charing Cross (Trafalgar Square) – Hendon (Bell)

14   Daily   Hornsey Rise (Favourite) – Putney Station

15   Weekdays   Putney Common (Cricketers) – East Ham (Duke's Head)
          Sundays   Putney Common (Cricketers) – Plaistow (Abbey Arms)

16   Daily   Victoria Station - Cricklewood (Crown)

17   Weekdays   South Ealing (New Inn) – London Bridge Station
          Sundays   Ealing Broadway (Railway Hotel) – East Ham (Duke's Head)

18   Weekdays   Kensal Green (Masons' Arms) – Clapham Common (Plough)
          Sundays   Stonebridge Park (Coach & Horses) – Clapham Common (Plough)

19   Daily   Clapham Junction (Northcote) - Highbury Barn (Tavern)

20   Weekdays   Hammersmith Broadway – West Norwood (Rosendale)
          Sundays   Putney Station – West Norwood (Rosendale)

21   Daily   Newington Green – Deptford Broadway

22   Weekdays   Homerton (Clapton Park Tavern) – Putney Station

23   Weekdays   Acton Vale (King's Arms) – Barking (Westbury)
          Sundays   South Ealing (New Inn) – Rippleside (Ship & Shovel)

24   Daily   Hampstead Heath (South End Green) – Victoria Station

25   Daily   Victoria Station – Old Ford (Lady Franklin)

26   Daily   West Kilburn (Falcon) – Hackney Wick

27   Weekdays   Richmond (Queen's Head) – Stoke Newington (Birdcage)
          Sundays   Turnham Green Church – Stoke Newington (Birdcage)

28   Daily   Wandsworth Bridge (Tavern) – West Hampstead (West End Green)

29   Daily   Victoria Station – Wood Green (Fishmongers' Arms)

30   Daily   Kings Cross Station – Putney Station

31   Daily   Chelsea (Stanley Arms) – Finchley Road Station (Met.)

32   Daily   Charing Cross (Trafalgar Square) – Shepherds Bush

33 – 34   *Numbers not in use*

35   Daily   Elephant & Castle – Walthamstow (Hoe Street Station)

36   Daily   West Kilburn (Falcon) – Liverpool Street Station

37 – 50   *Numbers not in use*

51   Sundays   Somerset House – Hampton Court via Putney, Richmond and Kingston

52   *Number not in use*

53   Sundays   North Finchley (Swan & Pyramids) – Ebury Bridge (Monster)

54   Sundays   Marble Arch – Leyton (Bakers' Arms)

55   Sundays   Elephant & Castle – Buckhurst Hill (Bald Faced Stag)

56   Sundays   Elephant & Castle – Epping Forest (Warren Wood House)

57   Sundays   Richmond (Queen's Head) – Shoreditch Church

> *NOTE: The Sunday extensions to Routes 17 and 23 and the Sunday routes 51, 53 to 57 operated during the winter months of 1911-1912 but were 'subject to suspension in the event of inclement weather' according to the L.G.O.C. maps.*

(b)   Other Operators

   (i)   British Automobile Development Ltd. ('British')

   Daily   Liverpool Street Station – Victoria Station

   (ii)   London and North Western Railway Company

   Weekdays   North Watford (Callowlands, Buckingham Road) – Croxley Green (Yorke Road)

   Weekdays   Watford Junction Station – Harrow & Wealdstone Station

   Weekdays   Harrow & Wealdstone Station – Harrow (Post Office)

   (iii)   London Central Omnibus Company Ltd.

   Daily   Chalk Farm (Adelaide) – Camberwell Green

   Weekdays   Richmond – Thames Ditton (Angel)
   Sundays   Kew Bridge – Thames Ditton (Angel)

   Daily   Kingston (Market Place) – Esher (Bear)

   (iv)   Metropolitan Steam Omnibus Company Ltd.

   Daily   Chelsea (Lots Road) – Camden Town Station (Und.)

   Daily   Fulham (Salisbury) – Brixton (Lambeth Town Hall)

   Weekdays(?)   Chelsea (Lots Road) – Shoreditch Church

   (v)   National Steam Car Company

   Daily   Shepherds Bush (White Horse) – Peckham Rye (King's Arms)

   Daily   Victoria Station – Liverpool Street Station

   Weekdays   Shepherds Bush (Victoria Tavern) – Liverpool Street Station

   Daily   Liverpool Street Station – Peckham (Rye Lane)

   (vi)   Park Langley Estate

   Daily (?)   Beckenham Junction Station – Park Langley Estate (Whitecroft Way) *(residents only)*
                  Operated by Commercial Cab Hirers Ltd.

(vii) <u>Thomas Tilling Ltd.</u>

12   Weekdays Peckham Rye (King's Arms) – Turnham Green (Church). *Joint service with L.G.O.C.*

           Weekdays Bromley (Market Place) – Lewisham
           Sundays   Bromley (Market Place) – Oxford Circus

           Weekdays Sidcup (Black Horse) – Lewisham
           Sundays   Sidcup (Black Horse) – Oxford Circus

ALTERATIONS FROM 1ST JANUARY 1912 TO 31ST AUGUST 1912

NOTE: Public holidays during this period on which Sunday services usually operated were 05.04.1912 (Good Friday), 08.04.1912 (Easter Monday), 27.05.1912 (Whit Monday) and 05.08.1912 (August Bank Holiday Monday).

(i)   <u>L.G.O.C.</u>

01.01.1912	**32**	Daily	Extended daily from Charing Cross (Trafalgar Square) to operate from Elephant & Castle via London Road, Waterloo Road, Waterloo Bridge, Wellington Street*, Strand to Trafalgar Square and line of route.
11.01.1912	**32**	Daily	Extended daily from Elephant & Castle to operate from Tower Bridge (Tooley Street) via Tower Bridge Road, New Kent Road to Elephant & Castle and line of route.
.02.1912(?)	**27**	Daily	Extended on Sundays from Turnham Green Church to operate from Richmond (Queen's Head) via Mondays to Saturdays route.
10.03.1912	**32**	Daily	Last day of operation on Sundays.
13.03.1912	**32**	Weekdays	Last day of operation between Tower Bridge (Tooley Street) and Charing Cross (Trafalgar Square) and between Ladbroke Grove and Shepherds Bush and re-routed at Ladbroke Grove to terminate at Ladbroke Grove (Eagle).
13.03.1912	**36**	Daily	Last day of operation between Victoria Station and Liverpool Street Station. (See Route 34).
14.03.1912	**33**	Daily	New Route: Liverpool Street Station (Mondays to Saturdays) or Piccadilly Circus (Sundays) – East Sheen (Black Horse) via New Broad Street*, Old Broad Street, Threadneedle Street (return via Princes Street, Moorgate Street*, London Wall, Blomfield Street, Liverpool Street), Bank, Queen Victoria Street, Cannon Street, St. Paul's Churchyard, Ludgate Hill, Fleet Street, Strand, Trafalgar Square (south side), Cockspur Street, Haymarket, Piccadilly Circus, Piccadilly, Hyde Park Corner, Knightsbridge, Kensington Gore, Kensington Road, Kensington High Street, Kensington Road*, Hammersmith Road, Hammersmith Broadway, Hammersmith Bridge Road, Hammersmith Bridge, Castelnau, Rocks Lane, Barnes Common, Upper Richmond Road, Sheen Road. *NOTE: Original terminus at East Sheen may have been Derby Arms until July 1912.*
14.03.1912	**34**	Weekdays	New Route: Liverpool Street Station – Brixton (Prince of Wales) via New Broad Street*, Old Broad Street, Threadneedle Street (return Princes Street, Moorgate Street*, London Wall, Blomfield Street, Liverpool Street), Bank, King William Street, London Bridge, Borough High Street, Newington Causeway, Elephant & Castle, Newington Butts*, Kennington Park Road, Brixton Road. (see Route 36).
30.03.1912			*Twickenham garage (AB) opened.*

| 30.03.1912 | **27** | Daily | Extended daily from Richmond (Queen's Head) to operate from Twickenham Station via London Road, York Street, Richmond Road, Richmond Bridge, Hill Street, George Street. (Terminal working via Richmond Green discontinued). |

| 30.03.1912 | **37** | Daily | New Route: Herne Hill (Half Moon Hotel) – Isleworth Market Place (Northumberland Arms) via Dulwich Road, Water Lane*, Effra Road, Acre Lane, Clapham Park Road, The Pavement, Clapham Common North Side, Battersea Rise, St. John's Road, St. John's Hill, East Hill, Wandsworth High Street, West Hill, Upper Richmond Road, Sheen Road, George Street, Hill Street, Richmond Bridge, Richmond Road, St. Margaret's Road*, South Street, Upper Square, Swan Street, Lower Square. |

04.1912 — *The April 1912 LGOC Bus Map gives a detailed diagram of operation of routes at Piccadilly Circus. At this time both Lower Regent Street and Haymarket carried two way traffic and all other sources indicate that routes between Piccadilly Circus and Trafalgar Square were split between the two roads and northbound buses returned by whichever road was used southbound. However the diagram in this map clearly marks Routes 3, 13, 20 and 32 as running south via Haymarket and Routes 6, 9, 12, 15 and 33 via Lower Regent Street but only Route 12 is shown as running northbound via Lower Regent Street, all the other routes are shown northbound via Haymarket. This diagram wasn't continued in later maps and no record can be found of how long this situation continued.*

| 01.04.1912 | **4** | Daily | New Route: Muswell Hill Broadway – Victoria Station via Muswell Hill Road*, Archway Road, Junction Road, Fortess Road, Kentish Town Road, Camden Town High Street*, Hampstead Road, Tottenham Court Road, Charing Cross Road, St. Martins Place, Trafalgar Square (east side), Whitehall, Parliament Street, Parliament Square, Broad Sanctuary, Victoria Street, Buckingham Palace Road (return via Wilton Road).. *NOTE: 'Muswell Hill Record' gives start date as 03.04.1912.* |

| 05.04.1912 | **5** | Daily | Re-extended on Sundays from Putney Station to Wimbledon (Rose & Crown) via Putney Hill, Putney Heath (east side)*, Parkside. |

| 05.04.1912 | **30** | Daily | Extended on Sundays from Putney Station to Twickenham Station via Upper Richmond Road, Sheen Road, George Street, Hill Street, Richmond Bridge, Richmond Road, York Street, London Road. |

| 05.04.1912 | **35** | Daily | Extended on Sundays from Walthamstow (Hoe Street Station) to Chingford Mount (Prince Albert) via Hoe Street, Chingford Road, Chingford Mount Road.. |

| 05.04.1912 | **52** | Sundays | Route Re-instated: (last ran 08.10.1911) Somerset House – Hampton Court (Vrow Walk) via Strand, Trafalgar Square (south side), Cockspur Street, Haymarket(?), Piccadilly Circus, Piccadilly, Hyde Park Corner, Knightsbridge, Kensington Gore, Kensington Road, Kensington High Street, Kensington Road*, Hammersmith Road, Hammersmith Broadway, King Street, Chiswick High Road, Kew Bridge, Kew Road, The Quadrant, George Street, Hill Street, Richmond Bridge, Richmond Road, York Street, King Street, Cross Deep, Waldegrave Road, Shacklegate Road*, Church Road, The Causeway, Park Road, Chestnut Avenue, Hampton Court Road. |

| 05.04.1912 | **54** | Sundays | Extended on Sundays from Leyton (Bakers' Arms) to Buckhurst Hill (Bald Faced Stag) via Lea Bridge Road, Whipps Cross, Forest Rise, Woodford New Road, Woodford High Road, Buckhurst Hill High Road. |

05.04.1912	**58**	Sundays	<u>New Route</u>: Charing Cross (Trafalgar Square) – Harrow Weald (Seven Balls) via St. Martins Place, Charing Cross Road, Tottenham Court Road, Euston Road, Marylebone Road*, Chapel Street, Edgware Road, Maida Vale, Kilburn High Road, Shoot-up Hill, Cricklewood Broadway, Edgware Road, West Hendon Broadway, Edgware Road*, Edgware High Street, Edgware Road*, Stanmore New Road*, Stanmore Broadway, Church Road, Station Road, Gordon Avenue.
05.04.1912	**59**	Sundays	<u>New Route</u>: Oxford Circus – South Croydon (Red Deer) via Regent Street, Piccadilly Circus, Haymarket, Cockspur Street, Whitehall, Parliament Street, Bridge Street, Westminster Bridge, Westminster Bridge Road, Kennington Road, Kennington Park Road, Brixton Road, Brixton Hill, Streatham Hill, Streatham High Road, London Road, North End, Croydon High Street, South End, Brighton Road.
21.04.1912	**18**	Daily	Last day of operation on Sundays between Stonebridge Park (Coach & Horses) and Craven Park.
22.04.1912	**14**	Daily	Extended daily from Hornsey Rise (Favourite) to operate from Wood Green (Turnpike Lane, The Wellington) via Turnpike Lane, Tottenham Lane, Crouch End Broadway, Crouch End Hill, Hornsey Rise to Hornsey Road and line of route.
22.04.1912	**18**	Daily	Extended daily from Kensal Green (Masons' Arms) to operate from Willesden (White Hart) via Church Road, Craven Park Road, High Street Harlesden, Harrow Road and line of route.
25.04.1912	**1**	Daily	Extended daily from Tower Bridge Road (Bricklayers' Arms) to Tower Bridge (Tooley Street) via Tower Bridge Road. Also extended Mondays to Saturdays from Cricklewood (L.G.O.C. Garage) and on Sundays from Hendon (Upper Welsh Harp) to operate from West Hendon (Station Road) via West Hendon Broadway, Edgware Road.
25.04.1912	**2**	Daily	Extended daily from Childs Hill (Castle) to Golders Green Station via Finchley Road.
29.04.1912	**21**	Daily	Extended from Deptford Broadway to Greenwich Park (Gloucester) via Deptford Bridge, Greenwich Road*, London Street*, Nelson Street*, King William Street* (return via Silver Street*, Stockwell Street).
29.04.1912	**34**	Weekdays	Withdrawn between Brixton Road and Brixton (Prince of Wales) and re-routed daily at Brixton Road to operate to Gipsy Hill (Paxton) via Atlantic Road, Railton Road, Norwood Road, Croxted Road, South Croxted Road.
.05.1912	**13**	Daily	<u>Additional Service</u> introduced on Saturdays and Sundays: Golders Green Station – Hendon (Church End, The Greyhound) via Golders Green Road, Brent Street, Church Road, Church End.
09.05.1912	**50**	Weekdays	<u>New Route</u>: Shepherds Bush (Bush Hotel) – Liverpool Street Station via Uxbridge Road, Holland Park Avenue, High Street Notting Hill Gate*, Bayswater Road, Marble Arch, Oxford Street, New Oxford Street, High Holborn, Holborn, Holborn Viaduct, Newgate Street, Cheapside, Bank, Princes Street, Moorgate Street*, London Wall, Blomfield Street, Liverpool Street (return via New Broad Street*, Old Broad Street, Threadneedle Street).
15.05.1912			*Under a new agreement with the L.G.O.C. of this date all Thomas Tilling Ltd. motor bus services were now operated in co-operation with the L.G.O.C. and during 1912 all Tilling routes were numbered into the L.G.O.C. series and shown in the L.G.O.C. monthly maps and guides. From this point onwards therefore Tilling routes are included in this section as appropriate with a note indicating Tilling operation. See also under Thomas Tilling in Section (b) below.*

23.05.1912	**11**	Daily	Extended Mondays to Saturdays during opening hours of the Latin-British Exhibition at White City and all day on Sundays from Shepherds Bush to operate from Wormwood Scrubs via Wood Lane.
23.05.1912	**34**	Weekdays	Withdrawn between Herne Hill Station and Gipsy Hill (Paxton) and re-routed Mondays to Saturdays to operate to Tulse Hill (Tulse Hill Hotel) via Norwood Road.
23.05.1912	**39**	Weekdays	New Route: Victoria Station – Sidcup (Black Horse) via Vauxhall Bridge Road, Vauxhall Bridge, Bridgefoot, Kennington Lane, Harleyford Road, Kennington Oval, Harleyford Street, Camberwell New Road, Camberwell Green, Church Street*, Peckham Road, Peckham High Street, Queens Road, New Cross Road, Lewisham High Road*, Loampit Hill, Loampit Vale, Lewisham High Street, Lee Bridge, Lee High Road, Eltham Road, Eltham Hill, Eltham High Street, Foots Cray Road, *Worked by Thomas Tilling Ltd.*
25.05.1912	**1**	Daily	Extended on Saturday afternoon and Sundays from West Hendon (Station Road) to operate from Edgware (Royal Oak) via Edgware Road* and line of route.
03.06.1912	**40**	Daily	New Route: Elephant & Castle – Upton Park (Duke of Edinburgh) via Newington Causeway, Borough High Street, London Bridge, King William Street, Fenchurch Street, Aldgate, Aldgate High Street, Whitechapel High Street, Commercial Road East*, East India Dock Road, Barking Road, Green Street.
09.06.1912	**3**	Daily	Last day of operation on Sundays. (See Route 59).
16.06.1912	**59**	Sundays	Extended on Sundays from Oxford Circus to operate from Camden Town Station (Und.) via Park Street*, Albany Street, Great Portland Street, Margaret Street (return via Mortimer Street), Regent Street to Oxford Circus and line of route. (See Route 3).
16.06.1912	**60**	Sundays	New Route: Tottenham Court Road (Oxford Street) – Wealdstone (Red Lion) via Oxford Street, Marble Arch, Edgware Road, Harrow Road, High Street Harlesden, Craven Park Road, Craven Park, Harrow Road*, Wembley High Road, Watford Road, Sheepcote Road, Station Road, High Street Wealdstone.
16.06.1912	**61**	Sundays	New Route: Brixton (White Horse) – Whyteleafe (Tavern) via Brixton Road, Brixton Hill, Streatham Hill, Streatham High Road, London Road, North End, High Street Croydon, South End, Brighton Road, Godstone Road.
16.06.1912	**38**	Daily	New Route: Victoria Station – Leyton Green (Mondays to Saturdays) or Epping Forest (Rising Sun) (Sundays) via Wilton Road, Victoria Street (return via Buckingham Palace Road), Grosvenor Gardens (north side), Grosvenor Place, Hyde Park Corner, Piccadilly, Piccadilly Circus, Shaftesbury Avenue, Charing Cross Road, New Oxford Street, Hart Street*, Vernon Place, Theobalds Road, Rosebery Avenue, St. John Street, Islington High Street, Upper Street, Essex Road, Balls Pond Road, Dalston Lane, Graham Road, Mare Street, Lower Clapton Road, Lea Bridge Road, Leyton High Road (Weekdays) or Lea Bridge Road, Whipps Cross, Forest Rise, Woodford New Road (Sundays).
20.06.1912(?)			*Leyton garage (T) opened.*
20.06.1912	**4**	Daily	Extended daily from Victoria Station to Pimlico (Gun) via Wilton Road, Denbigh Street, Lupus Street, Glasgow Terrace* (return via Grosvenor Road, Claverton Street).

20.06.1912	**8**	Daily	Withdrawn between Bank and Seven Kings (Seven Kings Hotel) and re-routed daily at Bank to operate to Old Ford (Lady Franklin) via Threadneedle Street, Bishopsgate, Norton Folgate, Shoreditch High Street, Bethnal Green Road, Green Street*, Roman Road, St. Stephen's Road, Old Ford Road. (See Route 25). Also extended daily from Willesden (White Hart) to operate from Willesden (White Horse) via Church Road and line of route.
20.06.1912	**25**	Daily	Withdrawn between Bank and Old Ford (Lady Franklin) and re-routed daily at Bank to operate to Seven Kings (Seven Kings Hotel) via Cornhill, Leadenhall Street, Aldgate, Aldgate High Street, Whitechapel High Street, Whitechapel Road, Mile End Road, Bow Road, Stratford High Street, Stratford Broadway, Romford Road, Ilford Hill, Ilford High Road, Seven Kings High Road. (See Route 8).
20.06.1912	**36**	Daily	Extended daily from Victoria Station to Catford (St. Laurence Church) via Vauxhall Bridge Road, Vauxhall Bridge, Bridgefoot, Kennington Lane, Harleyford Road, Kennington Oval, Harleyford Street, Camberwell New Road, Church Street*, Peckham Road, Peckham High Street, Queens Road, New Cross Road, Lewisham High Road*, Loampit Hill, Loampit Vale, Lewisham High Street, Rushey Green. *Becomes a joint operation with Thomas Tilling Ltd. on Mondays to Saturdays but L.G.O.C. only on Sundays.*
20.06.1912	**39**	Weekdays	Introduced on Sundays. *L.G.O.C. operation introduced daily, Thomas Tilling Ltd. remaining weekdays only.*
20.06.1912	**41**	Weekdays	New Route: Tufnell Park (Tufnell Park Hotel) – Old Ford (Lady Franklin) via Tufnell Park Road, Brecknock Road, York Road*, Grays Inn Road, Holborn, Holborn Viaduct, Cheapside, Bank, Threadneedle Street, Bishopsgate, Norton Folgate, Shoreditch High Street, Bethnal Green Road, Green Street*, Roman Road, St. Stephen's Road, Old Ford Road.
24.06.1912	**50**	Weekdays	Extended Mondays to Saturdays from Shepherds Bush (Bush Hotel) to operate from Willesden Junction via High Street Harlesden, Harrow Road, Scrubs Lane, Wood Lane to Shepherds Bush Green and line of route.
01.07.1912	**21**	Daily	Re-extended daily from Newington Green to operate from Wood Green (Fishmongers' Arms) via Green Lanes, Jolly Butchers Hill, Wood Green High Road, Green Lanes to Newington Green and line of route.
01.07.1912	**29**	Daily	Extended daily from Wood Green (Fishmongers' Arms) to Southgate (Cherry Tree) via Green Lanes, Aldermans Hill, Cannon Hill.
02.07.1912	**44**	Daily	New Route: Ealing Broadway Station – Northfields (Plough) via Haven Green, Castlebar Road, Eaton Rise, Montpelier Road West*, Castlebar Hill, Cleveland Road, Argyle Road, Drayton Green Road, Northfield Lane*.
04.07.1912	**14**	Daily	Last day of operation between Wood Green (Turnpike Lane, Wellington) and Hornsey Rise (Favourite). *Withdrawn due to weight restriction imposed on the Great Northern Railway bridge over Crouch End Station.*
07.07.1912	**29**	Daily	Extended on Sundays from Southgate (Cherry Tree) to Hadley Woods (Cock Inn) via High Street Southgate, Chase Side, Cockfosters Road, Chalk Lane.
14.07.1912	**45**	Daily	New Route: Harlington Corner (Coach & Horses) – Staines (Police Station) via Bath Road, Wellington Road, Staines Road, London Road, High Street Staines.

14.07.1912	**62**	Sundays	New Route: Hounslow (Bell) – Windsor Castle via Bath Road*, Colnbrook High Street, Bath Road*, Sussex Place, High Street Slough, Windsor Road, Slough Road, Eton High Street, Windsor Bridge, Thames Street, High Street Windsor.
15.07.1912	**46**	Weekdays	New Route: (Supplemental service to Route 16) Victoria Station – Kilburn Station (L.& N.W.R.) via Wilton Road, Victoria Street (return via Buckingham Palace Road), Grosvenor Gardens (north side), Grosvenor Place, Hyde Park Corner, Hamilton Place, Park Lane, Marble Arch, Edgware Road, Maida Vale, Kilburn High Road.
By 17.07.1912	**58**	Sundays	By implication the terminal at Harrow Weald moved from 'Seven Balls' to 'Red Lion'. *A meeting of the Hendon Rural District Council on 17.05.1912 reported a letter from the L.G.O.C. stating that a future route would be via Bamford Corner (now Brockhurst Corner), Kenton Lane returning via Gordon Avenue. A press report of a further meeting of the Council on 17.07.1912 states there was cause for complaint of obstruction by motor buses from Charing Cross to the 'Red Lion' at Harrow Weald thereat. Since this presumably refers to Route 58, it implies a change of terminal and a re-routing away from Kenton Lane.*
18.07.1912 (?)			*Chelverton Road, Putney garage (AF) opened.*
20.07.1912	**4**	Daily	Re-routed daily between Muswell Hill Broadway and Highgate Station (G.N.R.) to operate via Muswell Hill Road*, Fortis Green Road*, High Road East Finchley, Great North Road, Archway Road and line of route instead of via Muswell Hill Road.
20.07.1912	**47**	Daily	New Route: Shoreditch Church – Bromley (Market Place) via Shoreditch High Street, Norton Folgate, Bishopsgate, Gracechurch Street, King William Street, London Bridge, Duke Street Hill, Tooley Street, Dockhead*, Parker's Row*, Jamaica Road, Union Road*, Lower Road, Evelyn Street, High Street Deptford, Deptford Broadway, Brookmill Road, Thurston Road, Loampit Vale, Lewisham High Street, Rushey Green, Bromley Road*, Bromley Hill, London Road, High Street Bromley. *Operated by Thomas Tilling Ltd.*
21.07.1912	**63**	Sundays	Previously unnumbered Thomas Tilling Ltd. route numbered 63: Sidcup (Black Horse) – Oxford Circus via Foots Cray Road, Eltham High Street, Eltham Hill, Eltham Green, Eltham Road, Lee High Road, Lee Bridge, Lewisham High Street, Loampit Vale, Loampit Hill, Lewisham High Road*, New Cross Road, Queens Road, Peckham High Street, Peckham Road, Church Street*, Camberwell Green, Camberwell Road, Walworth Road*, Elephant & Castle, St. George's Road, Westminster Bridge Road, Westminster Bridge, Bridge Street, Parliament Street, Whitehall, Cockspur Street, Pall Mall, Waterloo Place, Lower Regent Street, Piccadilly Circus, Regent Street. *Operated by Thomas Tilling Ltd.*
21.07.1912	**64**	Sundays	Previously unnumbered Thomas Tilling Ltd. route numbered 64: Bromley (Market Place) – Oxford Circus via London Road, Bromley Road*, Rushey Green, Lewisham High Street, Loampit Vale, Loampit Hill, Lewisham High Road*, New Cross Road, Queens Road, Peckham High Street, Peckham Road, Church Street*, Camberwell Green, Camberwell Road, Walworth Road*, Elephant & Castle, St. George's Road, Westminster Bridge Road, Westminster Bridge, Bridge Street, Parliament Street, Whitehall, Cockspur Street, Pall Mall, Waterloo Place, Lower Regent Street, Piccadilly Circus, Regent Street. *Operated by Thomas Tilling Ltd.*
22.07.1912(?)			*Palmers Green garage (AD) opened.*
25.07.1912	**42**	Daily	New Route: Finsbury Park Station – Clapton Pond via Seven Sisters Road, Amhurst Park, Clapton Common, Upper Clapton Road.

27.07.1912	**35**	Daily	Extended on Mondays to Saturdays from Walthamstow (Hoe Street Station) to Walthamstow (Crooked Billet) via Hoe Street, Chingford Road.
28.07.1912	**35**	Daily	Extended on Sundays from Elephant & Castle to operate from Brixton (George Canning) via Effra Road, Brixton Road, Kennington Park Road, Newington Butts* to Elephant & Castle and line of route.
28.07.1912	**62**	Sundays	Last day of operation (introduced daily and renumbered 81).
31.07.1912	**44**	Daily	Last day of operation (renumbered 80).
31.07.1912	**45**	Daily	Last day of operation (re-routed and renumbered 82).
01.08.1912	**80**	Daily	Route 44 renumbered 80: Ealing Broadway Station – Northfields (Plough) via Haven Green, Castlebar Road, Eaton Rise, Montpelier Road West*, Castlebar Hill, Cleveland Road, Argyle Road, Drayton Green Road, Northfield Lane*.
01.08.1912	**81**	Daily	Route 62 introduced daily and renumbered 81: Hounslow (Bell) – Windsor Castle via Bath Road*, Colnbrook High Street, Bath Road*, Sussex Place, High Street Slough, Windsor Road, Slough Road, Eton High Street, Windsor Bridge, Thames Street, High Street Windsor.
01.08.1912	**82**	Daily	Route 45 re-routed *[but see below]* via Feltham and renumbered 82: Harlington Corner (Coach & Horses) – Staines (Police Station) via Bath Road, Wellington Road, Staines Road, Hounslow Road, Feltham High Street, Ashford Road, Church Road, Stanwell Road, London Road, Staines High Street. *{NOTE: Although this re-routeing is shown in the Bus Maps for September and October 1912, it is doubtful if it actually occurred due to a weak railway bridge en-route. No tickets for the route via Feltham were ever issued and the December map reverts to the direct route via Staines Road].*
02.08.1912	**48**	Daily	New Route: Wood Green (Turnpike Lane, Wellington) – Strand (Aldwych) via Green Lanes, West Green Road, High Road Tottenham, Stamford Hill, High Street Stoke Newington, Stoke Newington Road, Kingsland High Street, Kingsland Road, Old Street, Clerkenwell Road, Grays Inn Road, Holborn, Chancery Lane, Fleet Street, Strand.
03.08.1912	**13**	Daily	Additional service on Saturdays and Sundays between Golders Green Station and Hendon (Church End, Greyhound) transferred to Route 83.
03.08.1912	**43**	Daily	New Route: Highgate Station (Und.) (Archway Tavern) – London Bridge Station via Holloway Road, Upper Street, Islington High Street, City Road, Finsbury Pavement, Moorgate Street*, Princes Street, Bank, King William Street, London Bridge.
03.08.1912	**55**	Sundays	Introduced on Saturdays Elephant & Castle – Buckhurst Hill (Bald Faced Stag) as on Sundays.
03.08.1912	**83**	Daily	New Route: Golders Green Station – Hendon (Church End, Greyhound) via Golders Green Road, Brent Street, Church Road, Church End.
03.08.1912	**84**	Sats & Suns	New Route: Golders Green Station – St. Albans (Rising Sun) via Finchley Road, Regents Park Road, Ballards Lane, High Road North Finchley, Whetstone High Road, Great North Road, Barnet Hill, Barnet High Street, New Road*, St. Albans Road, Ridge Hill, St. Albans Road, Barnet Road, London Colney High Street, London Road, Chequer Street, St. Peter's Street (return via Market Place, High Street except on market days)..

03.08.1912	**85**	Daily	New Route: Putney Bridge Station – Roehampton (Earl Spencer) extended on Sundays to Kingston Hill (Tram Terminus) via Ranelagh Gardens, High Street Fulham (return via Gonville Street, Station Approach), Putney Bridge, Putney High Street, Putney Hill, Portsmouth Road*, Putney Heath (north side), Treville Street, Medfield Street, Roehampton Lane, Kingston Road, Roehampton Vale, Kingston Vale, Kingston Hill.
12.08.1912	**86**	Daily	New Route: Barking Station – Barkingside (Maypole) via Longbridge Road*, Fanshawe Avenue, Ilford Lane, Cranbrook Road, Barkingside High Street, Fencepiece Road.
18.08.1912	**4**	Daily	Last day of operation. (See Routes 24, 43, 44, 87).
18.08.1912	**89**	Sundays	New Route: Hounslow (Bell) – Burnham Beeches (Wingrove's Tea Rooms) via Bath Road*, Colnbrook High Street, Bath Road*, Sussex Place, High Street Slough, Bath Road, Farnham Road, Beaconsfield Road, Kingsway, Beeches Road*, East Burnham Road*..
19.08.1912	**20**	Daily	Withdrawn between Putney Station (Sundays), Hammersmith (Weekdays) and Shepherds Bush Green and re-routed to operate daily from Shepherds Bush (Bush Hotel) via Uxbridge Road to Holland Park Avenue and line of route. (See Route 44).
19.08.1912	**24**	Daily	Extended daily from Victoria Station to Pimlico (Gun) via Wilton Road, Denbigh Street, Lupus Street, Glasgow Terrace* (return via Grosvenor Road, Claverton Street). (See Route 4).
19.08.1912	**43**	Daily	Extended daily from Highgate (Archway Tavern) to operate from Muswell Hill Broadway via Muswell Hill Road*, Fortis Green Road*, High Road East Fin chley, Great North Road, Archway Road to Holloway Road and line of route. (See Route 4).
19.08.1912	**44**	Daily	New Route: Highgate (Archway Tavern) – Putney Station via Junction Road, Fortess Road, Kentish Town Road, Park Street*, Albany Street, Great Portland Street, Margaret Street (return via Mortimer Street), Regent Street, Oxford Street, Marble Arch, Bayswater Road, High Street Notting Hill Gate*, Holland Park Avenue, Richmond Road*, Netherwood Road, Shepherds Bush Road, Brook Green Road*, Hammersmith Broadway, Queen Street*, Fulham Palace Road, Fulham High Street, Putney Bridge, Putney High Street. (See Routes 4, 20).
19.08.1912	**87**	Daily	New Route: Colney Hatch Lane (Wilton Road) – Highgate (Archway Tavern) via Colney Hatch Lane*, Muswell Hill Broadway, Muswell Hill Road*, Fortis Green Road*, High Road East Finchley, Great North Road, Archway Road. (See Route 4)
19.08.1912	**88**	Daily	New Route: Finsbury Park Station – Clapton Pond via Blackstock Road, Brownswood Road, Lordship Park, Manor Road, Stamford Hill, Northwold Road, Upper Clapton Road.
26.08.1912	**4**	Daily	New Route: Finsbury Park Station – Elephant & Castle via Blackstock Road, Highbury Park, Highbury Grove, St. Paul's Road, Upper Street, Islington High Street, Goswell Road, Aldersgate Street, St. Paul's Churchyard, Ludgate Hill, New Bridge Street, Blackfriars Bridge, Blackfriars Road, London Road.
26.08.1912	**42**	Daily	Extended daily from Clapton Pond to Tower of London via Lower Clapton Road, Mare Street, Cambridge Road*, Whitechapel Road, Whitechapel High Street, Aldgate High Street, Minories.

26.08.1912	**49**	Daily	New Route: Camden Town Station (Und.) – Clapham Junction via Park Street*, Albert Road*, St. John's Wood Road, Lisson Grove, Marylebone Road*, Chapel Street, Praed Street, Eastbourne Terrace, Bishops Road*, Queens Road*, Bayswater Road, High Street Notting Hill Gate*, Church Street*, Kensington Road, Palace Gate, Gloucester Road, Harrington Road, Cranley Terrace*, Onslow Square, Sydney Place, Fulham Road, Sydney Street, Kings Road, Oakley Street, Cheyne Walk, Battersea Bridge, Battersea Bridge Road, Battersea Park Road, Falcon Road.
28.08.1912	**50**	Weekdays	Last day of operation between Willesden Junction and Shepherds Bush (Bush Hotel). (See Route 66).
29.08.1912	**66**	Daily	New Route: Willesden† - Tooting (Mitre) via High Street Harlesden, Harrow Road, Scrubs Lane, Wood Lane, The Lawn*, Shepherds Bush Road, Brook Green Road*, Hammersmith Broadway, Queen Street*, Fulham Palace Road, Fulham High Street, Putney Bridge, Putney High Street, Upper Richmond Road, West Hill, Wandsworth High Street, Garratt Lane, Defoe Road*, Tooting Broadway, Mitcham Road. (See Route 50).

† NOTE: The L.G.O.C. map for September 1912 shows the terminus at Willesden as 'Willesden Junction' but press publicity and tickets for the route indicate that the route operated from Pound Lane . From the times of first and last buses in that map the buses came from Chelverton Road garage. Willesden (Pound Lane) garage AC opened in October 1912. The L.G.O.C. map for October 1912 shows the 66 terminal as Pound Lane. The terminus at this spot had hitherto been 'White Hart'. Early in 1913, 66 was operated from AC with green Metropolitan Steam B-type buses. Throughout the period when the terminus of 66 was shown as Willesden (Pound Lane) in the list of routes, the terminus of 8 was shown as 'White Horse' and 18 as 'White Hart' but on the map there was only one terminal shown for all three routes which was obviously wrong. Photographs of 1912 B-type buses in General livery with AC codes show the destination board with only plain 'WILLESDEN'.

(b)   Other Operators

(i)   London Central Omnibus Company

03.01.1912			A new company – New Central Omnibus Company Ltd. – incorporated to acquire London Central Omnibus Company and their routes.

(ii) Metropolitan Steam Omnibus Company Ltd.

NOTE: Considerable research has failed to produced confirmation for many of the dates of alterations in the services of this operator. Those which are not confirmed are marked (?) and can be considered as approximate.

26.01.1912	Daily	Chelsea (Lots Road) – Camden Town route withdrawn.
26.02.1912	Weekdays(?)	Chelsea (Lots Road) – Shoreditch Church route extended weekdays(?) from Shoreditch Church to Dalston Junction via Kingsland Road.
11.03.1912	Daily	New Route: Chelsea (Lots Road) – Gipsy Hill (Paxton) via Kings Road, Beaufort Street (?), Battersea Bridge, Battersea Bridge Road, Battersea Park Road, Falcon Road, Lavender Hill, Cedars Road, Clapham Common North Side, The Pavement, Clapham Park Road, Acre Lane, Effra Road, Water Lane*, Dulwich Road, Norwood Road, Croxted Road, South Croxted Road.

07.04.1912	Daily	Route Re-instated: Petersham (Dysart Arms) – Brixton (Lambeth Town Hall) via Petersham Road, Lower Road*, Hill Street, George Street, Sheen Road, Upper Richmond Road, West Hill, Wandsworth High Street, East Hill, St. John's Hill, St. John's Road, Battersea Rise, Clapham Common North Side, Old Town, The Pavement, Clapham Park Road, Acre Lane.
22.04.1912(?)	Weekdays(?)	Last day of operation of the Chelsea (Lots Road) – Dalston Junction route.
23.04.1912	Daily	Chelsea (Lots Road) – Gipsy Hill (Paxton) route re-routed daily between Kings Road and Clapham Common to run via Harwood Road, The Broadway Walham Green*, Fulham Road, Fulham High Street, Putney Bridge, Putney High Street, Upper Richmond Road, West Hill, Wandsworth High Street, St. John's Hill, St. John's Road, Battersea Rise to Clapham Common North Side and line of route instead of via Beaufort Street (?), Battersea Bridge, Battersea Bridge Road, Battersea Park Road, Falcon Road, Lavender Hill, Cedars Road. *NOTE: Chelsea to Walham Green was probably only covered by garage workings, the normal terminus being Fulham (Salisbury).*
.06.1912		*The Annual Report of the Traffic Branch for 1912 (Royal Commission on London Traffic) lists the names of operators for the first time. The only routes of Metropolitan Steam listed as operating during the first week of June 1912 were:*
		Fulham (Salisbury) – Gipsy Hill via Putney Petersham (Dysart Arms) – Brixton (Lambeth Town Hall) via Putney.
		Both were shown as daily in the accompanying map. Therefore all other routes may be regarded as withdrawn by this date.

(iii) National Steam Car Company Ltd.

25.02.1912	Daily	Victoria Station – Liverpool Street Station extended daily from Victoria Station to operate from Fulham (Salisbury) via Dawes Road, The Broadway Walham Green*, Fulham Road, Brompton Road, Sloane Street, Sloane Square, Lower Sloane Street, Pimlico Road, Buckingham Palace Road to Victoria Street and line of route.
14.03.1912	Daily(?)	New Route: Chalk Farm (Adelaide) – Peckham Rye (King's Arms) via Chalk Farm Road, Park Street*, Albany Street, Great Portland Street, Margaret Street (return via Mortimer Street), Regent Street, Piccadilly Circus, Lower Regent Street, Waterloo Place, Pall Mall, Cockspur Street, Whitehall, Parliament Street, Bridge Street, Westminster Bridge, Westminster Bridge Road, St. George's Road, Elephant & Castle, Walworth Road*, Camberwell Road, Camberwell Green, Church Street*, Peckham Road, Peckham High Street, Rye Lane.
05.(or 07?).04.1912	Sundays	New Route: Peckham Rye (King's Arms) – Hampton Court via Rye Lane, Peckham High Street, Peckham Road, Church Street*, Camberwell Green, Denmark Hill, Coldharbour Lane, Gresham Road, Brixton Road, Acre Lane, Clapham Park Road, Clapham Common (south side), Balham Hill, Balham High Road, Upper Tooting Road, Tooting High Street, Colliers Wood High Street, Merton High Street, Merton Road, Wimbledon Broadway, Worple Road, Pepys Road, Coombe Road, West Barnes Lane, Burlington Road, Kingston Road, Cambridge Road, London Road, Clarence Street, Kingston Bridge, Hampton Court Road.
.05.1912	Sundays	New Route: Peckham Rye (King's Arms) – Kew Green via Rye Lane, Peckham High Street, Peckham Road, Church Street*, Camberwell Green, Camberwell Road, Walworth Road*, Elephant & Castle, St. George's Road, Westminster Bridge Road, Westminster Bridge, Bridge Street, Parliament Street, Whitehall, Cockspur Street, Pall Mall, Waterloo

		Place, Lower Regent Street, Piccadilly Circus, Piccadilly, Hyde Park Corner, Knightsbridge, Kensington Gore, Kensington Road, Kensington High Street, Kensington Road*, Hammersmith Road, Hammersmith Broadway, King Street, Chiswick High Road, Kew Bridge.
.05.1912 (?)	Daily	Liverpool Street Station – Peckham (Rye Lane) route extended on Sundays from Peckham to Peckham Rye (King's Arms) via Rye Lane and re-routed on Sundays at Gracechurch Street to operate from Stratford Broadway via Stratford High Street, Bow Road, Mile End Road, Whitechapel Road, Whitechapel High Street, Aldgate High Street, Aldgate, Fenchurch Street to Gracechurch Street and line of route.
23.06.1912	Sundays	Route Re-instated: Sidcup (Black Horse) – Oxford Circus via Foots Cray Road, Eltham High Street, Eltham Hill, Eltham Green, Eltham Road, Lee High Road, Lee Bridge, Lewisham High Street, Loampit Vale, Loampit Hill, Lewisham High Road*, New Cross Road, Queens Road, Peckham High Street, Peckham Road, Church Street*, Camberwell Green, Camberwell Road, Walworth Road*, Elephant & Castle, St. George's Road, Westminster Bridge Road, Westminster Bridge, Bridge Street, Parliament Street, Whitehall, Cockspur Street, Pall Mall, Waterloo Place, Lower Regent Street, Piccadilly Circus, Regent Street.
21.07.1912	Sundays	Last day of operation of the Oxford Circus – Sidcup (Black Horse) route.
28.07.1912	Sundays	New Route: Oxford Circus – Bexley (King's Head) via Regent Street, Piccadilly Circus, Lower Regent Street, Waterloo Place, Pall Mall, Cockspur Street, Whitehall, Parliament Street, Bridge Street, Westminster Bridge, Westminster Bridge Road, St .George's Road, Elephant & Castle, Walworth Road*, Camberwell Road, Camberwell Green, Church Street*, Peckham Road, Peckham High Street, Queens Road, New Cross Road, Lewisham High Road*, Loampit Hill, Loampit Vale, Lewisham High Street, Lee Bridge, Lee High Road, Eltham Road, Eltham Green, Eltham Hill, Eltham High Street, Bexley Road, Blackfen Road, Blendon Road, Bridgen Road, Park Hill Road, High Street Bexley.
28.08.1912	Daily	Fulham (Salisbury) – Liverpool Street Station route re-routed daily between Brompton Road and Trafalgar Square via Knightsbridge, Hyde Park Corner, Piccadilly, Piccadilly Circus, Haymarket(?), Cockspur Street to Trafalgar Square and line of route instead of via Sloane Street, Sloane Square, Lower Sloane Street, Pimlico Road, Buckingham Palace Road, Victoria Street, Broad Sanctuary, Parliament Square, Parliament Street, Whitehall.

(iv) New Central Omnibus Company Ltd.

03.01.1912		*A new company – New Central Omnibus Company Ltd. – incorporated to acquire London Central Omnibus Company and their routes.*
07.04.1912	Sundays	Former London Central Omnibus Company route re-instated as: Waterloo Station – Hampton Court (Vrow Walk) via Waterloo Bridge, Lancaster Place, Strand, Trafalgar Square, Piccadilly, Hyde Park Corner, Knightsbridge, Kensington Gore, Kensington Road, Kensington High Street, Hammersmith Road, Hammersmith Broadway, King Street, Chiswick High Road, Kew Bridge, Kew Road, George Street, Hill Street Richmond, Richmond Bridge, Richmond Road, York Street, King Street, Cross Deep, Waldegrave Road, Shacklegate Road*, Church Road, The Causeway, Park Road, Chestnut Avenue, Hampton Court Road.

(v)   Park Langley Estate Service

During 05.1912	Daily(?)	*The contract was taken over by H.Taylor of Beckenham.*

(vi) Thomas Tilling Ltd.

15.05.1912   *Under a new agreement with the L.G.O.C. of this date all Thomas Tilling
                    Ltd. motor bus services were now operated in co-operation with the
                    L.G.O.C. and during 1912 all Tilling routes were numbered into the
                    L.G.O.C. series and shown in the L.G.O.C. monthly maps and guides.
                    From this point onwards therefore Tilling routes are included in the
                    L.G.O.C. section as appropriate with a note indicating Tilling operation.
                    The transition of the Tilling routes existing as at this date is shown below
                    (see L.G.O.C. section for details).*

12   Weekdays Peckham Rye (King's Arms) – Turnham Green (Church) continued. *(Joint service with
                    L.G.O.C.)*

          Weekdays Bromley (Market Place) – Lewisham absorbed into new Route 47 on 20.07.1912.

          Sundays   Bromley (Market Place) – Oxford Circus numbered 64 on 21.07.1912.

          Weekdays Sidcup (Black Horse) – Lewisham extended and numbered 39 on 23.05.1912.

          Sundays   Sidcup (Black Horse) – Oxford Circus numbered 63 on 21.07.1912.

MOTOR OMNIBUS ROUTES AS AT SATURDAY 31ST AUGUST 1912

(a)   L.G.O.C. & Thomas Tilling Ltd.

1   Mons-Fris West Hendon (Station Road) – Tower Bridge (Tooley Street)
          &Sats a.m.
          Sats p.m. Edgware (Royal Oak) – Tower Bridge (Tooley Street)
          & Suns

2   Daily   Ebury Bridge (Monster) – Golders Green Station

3   Weekdays   Brixton (George Canning) – Camden Town Station (Und.)

4   Daily   Finsbury Park Station – Elephant & Castle

5   Weekdays   Stroud Green (Stapleton Hall Tavern) – Putney Station
          Sundays   Stroud Green (Stapleton Hall Tavern) – Wimbledon (Rose & Crown)

6   Weekdays   Kensal Rise Station – Shoreditch Church
          Sundays   Kensal Rise Station – Charing Cross (Trafalgar Square)

7   Daily   Wormwood Scrubs – Liverpool Street Station

8   Daily   Willesden (White Horse) – Old Ford (Lady Franklin)

9   Daily   Barnes (Avondale Road) – Liverpool Street Station

10   Daily   Wanstead (George) – Elephant & Castle

11   Daily†   Wormwood Scrubs – Liverpool Street Station
          † During weekdays runs Shepherds Bush – Liverpool Street Station only outside exhibition opening
                    hours at the Latin – British Exhibition at White City.

12   Daily   Turnham Green Church – Peckham Rye (King's Arms)
                    Joint operation by Thomas Tilling Ltd. & L.G.O.C. on weekdays. L.G.O.C. only on Sundays.

13   Weekdays   London Bridge Station – Hendon (Bell)
          Sundays   Charing Cross (Trafalgar Square) – Hendon (Bell)

14   Daily   Hornsey Rise (Favourite) – Putney Station

| 15 | Weekdays | Putney Common (Cricketers) – East Ham (Duke's Head) |
| | Sundays | Putney Common (Cricketers) – Plaistow (Abbey Arms) |

| 16 | Daily | Victoria Station – Cricklewood (Crown) |

| 17 | Weekdays | South Ealing (New Inn) – London Bridge Station |
| | Sundays | Ealing Broadway (Railway Hotel) – East Ham (Duke's Head) |

| 18 | Daily | Willesden (White Hart) – Clapham Common (Plough) |

| 19 | Daily | Clapham Junction (Northcote) – Highbury Barn (Tavern) |

| 20 | Daily | Shepherds Bush (Bush Hotel) – West Norwood (Rosendale) |

| 21 | Daily | Wood Green (Fishmongers' Arms) – Greenwich Park (Gloucester) |

| 22 | Weekdays | Homerton (Clapton Park Tavern) – Putney Station |

| 23 | Weekdays | Acton Vale (King's Arms) – Barking (Westbury) |
| | Sundays | South Ealing (New Inn) – Rippleside (Ship & Shovel) |

| 24 | Daily | Hampstead Heath (South End Green) – Pimlico (Gun) |

| 25 | Daily | Victoria Station – Seven Kings (Seven Kings Hotel) |

| 26 | Daily | West Kilburn (Falcon) – Hackney Wick |

| 27 | Daily | Twickenham Station – Stoke Newington (Birdcage) |

| 28 | Daily | Wandsworth Bridge (Tavern) – West Hampstead (West End Green) |

| 29 | Weekdays | Victoria Station – Southgate (Cherry Tree) |
| | Sundays | Victoria Station – Hadley Woods (Cock Inn) |

| 30 | Weekdays | Kings Cross Station – Putney Station |
| | Sundays | Kings Cross Station – Twickenham Station |

| 31 | Daily | Chelsea (Stanley Arms) – Finchley Road Station (Met.) |

| 32 | Weekdays | Charing Cross (Trafalgar Square) – Ladbroke Grove (Eagle) |

| 33 | Weekdays | Liverpool Street Station – East Sheen (Black Horse) |
| | Sundays | Piccadilly Circus – East Sheen (Black Horse) |

| 34 | Weekdays | Liverpool Street Station – Tulse Hill (Tulse Hill Hotel) |

| 35 | Weekdays | Elephant & Castle – Walthamstow (Crooked Billet) |
| | Sundays | Brixton (George Canning) – Chingford Mount (Prince Albert) |

| 36 | Daily | West Kilburn (Falcon) – Catford (St .Laurence Church) |
| | | *Joint operation by Thomas Tilling Ltd. & L.G.O.C. on weekdays. L.G.O.C. only on Sundays.* |

| 37 | Daily | Herne Hill (Half Moon Hotel) – Isleworth Market Place (Northumberland Arms) |

| 38 | Weekdays | Victoria Station – Leyton Green |
| | Sundays | Victoria Station – Epping Forest (Rising Sun) |

| 39 | Daily | Victoria Station – Sidcup (Black Horse) |
| | | *Joint operation by Thomas Tilling Ltd. & L.G.O.C. on weekdays. L.G.O.C. only on Sundays.* |

| 40 | Daily | Elephant & Castle – Upton Park (Duke of Edinburgh) |

| 41 | Weekdays | Tufnell Park (Tufnell Park Hotel) – Old Ford (Lady Franklin) |

42	Daily	Finsbury Park Station – Tower of London
43	Daily	Muswell Hill Broadway – London Bridge Station
44	Daily	Highgate (Archway Tavern) – Putney Station
45		*Number not in use*
46	Weekdays	Victoria Station – Kilburn Station (L.&N.W.R.)
47	Daily	Shoreditch Church – Bromley (Market Place) *Operated daily by Thomas Tilling Ltd.*
48	Daily	Wood Green (Turnpike Lane, Wellington) – Strand (Aldwych)
49	Daily	Camden Town Station (Und.) – Clapham Junction
50	Weekdays	Shepherds Bush (Bush Hotel) – Liverpool Street Station
51	Sundays	Somerset House – Hampton Court via Putney, Richmond and Kingston
52	Sundays	Somerset House – Hampton Court via Kew, Richmond, Teddington
53	Sundays	North Finchley (Swan & Pyramids) – Ebury Bridge (Monster)
54	Sundays	Marble Arch – Buckhurst Hill (Bald Faced Stag)
55	Sats & Suns	Elephant & Castle – Buckhurst Hill (Bald Faced Stag)
56	Sundays	Elephant & Castle – Epping Forest (Warren Wood House)
57	Sundays	Richmond (Queen's Head) – Shoreditch Church
58	Sundays	Charing Cross (Trafalgar Square) – Harrow Weald (Red Lion)
59	Sundays	Camden Town Station (Und.) – South Croydon (Red Deer)
60	Sundays	Tottenham Court Road (Oxford Street) – Wealdstone (Red Lion)
61	Sundays	Brixton (White Horse) – Whyteleafe (Tavern)
62		*Number not in use*
63	Sundays	Sidcup (Black Horse) – Oxford Circus *Operated Sundays by Thomas Tilling Ltd.*
64	Sundays	Bromley (Market Place) – Oxford Circus *Operated Sundays by Thomas Tilling Ltd.*
65		*Number not in use*
66	Daily	Willesden – Tooting (Mitre)
67 – 79		*Numbers not in use*
80	Daily	Ealing Broadway Station – Northfields (Plough)
81	Daily	Hounslow (Bell) – Windsor Castle
82	Daily	Harlington Corner (Coach & Horses) – Staines (Police Station)
83	Daily	Golders Green Station – Hendon (Church End, Greyhound)
84	Sats & Suns	Golders Green Station – St. Albans (Rising Sun)

85	Weekdays	Putney Bridge Station – Roehampton (Earl Spencer)
	Sundays	Putney Bridge Station – Kingston Hill (Tram Terminus)
86	Daily	Barking Station – Barkingside (Maypole)
87	Daily	Colney Hatch Lane (Wilton Road) – Highgate (Archway Tavern)
88	Daily	Finsbury Park Station – Clapton Pond
89	Sundays	Hounslow (Bell) – Burnham Beeches (Wingrove's Tea Rooms)

(b) Other Operators

(i) British Automobile Development Ltd. ('British')

Daily   Liverpool Street Station – Victoria Station

(ii) London and North Western Railway Company

Weekdays North Watford (Callowlands, Buckingham Road) – Croxley Green (Yorke Road)

Weekdays Watford Junction Station – Harrow & Wealdstone Station

Weekdays Harrow & Wealdstone Station – Harrow (Post Office)

(iii) Metropolitan Steam Omnibus Company Ltd.

Daily   Fulham (Salisbury) – Gipsy Hill (Paxton)

Daily   Petersham (Dysart Arms) – Brixton (Lambeth Town Hall)

(iv) National Steam Car Company

Daily   Shepherds Bush (White Horse) – Peckham Rye (King's Arms)

Weekdays Shepherds Bush (Victoria Tavern) – Liverpool Street Station

Daily   Fulham (Salisbury) – Liverpool Street Station

Weekdays Liverpool Street Station – Peckham (Rye Lane)
Sundays   Stratford Broadway – Peckham Rye (King's Arms)

Daily(?)   Chalk Farm (Adelaide) – Peckham Rye (King's Arms)

Sundays   Peckham Rye (King's Arms) – Hampton Court

Sundays   Peckham Rye (King's Arms) – Kew Green

Sundays   Oxford Circus – Bexley (King's Head)

(v) New Central Omnibus Company Ltd.

Daily   Chalk Farm (Adelaide) – Camberwell Green

Sundays   Waterloo Station – Hampton Court

Weekdays Richmond Station – Thames Ditton (Angel)
Sundays   Kew Bridge – Thames Ditton (Angel)

Daily   Kingston (Market Place) – Esher (Bear)

(vi) Park Langley Estate

Daily (?) Beckenham Junction Station – Park Langley Estate (Whitecroft Way) *(residents only)*
Operated under contract by H. Taylor of Beckenham Ltd.

ALTERATIONS FROM 1ST SEPTEMBER 1912 TO 31ST DECEMBER 1912

(a) L.G.O.C. and Thomas Tilling Ltd.

01.09.1912	**82**	Daily	Last day of operation between Harlington Corner (Coach & Horses) and Hounslow Barracks Station (Und)*.
02.09.1912	**83**	Daily	Withdrawn between Church Road and Hendon (Church End, Greyhound) and re-routed daily to West Hendon (Station Road) via The Burroughs, Station Road.
06.09.1912	**48**	Daily	Withdrawn between Wood Green (Turnpike Lane, Wellington) and High Road Tottenham and re-routed to operate daily from Tottenham (Swan) via Tottenham High Road and line of route. Also extended daily from Strand (Aldwych) to Stockwell (Swan) via Wellington Street*, Waterloo Bridge, Waterloo Road, Oakley Street*, Kennington Road, Kennington Park Road, Clapham Road.
09.09.1912	**34**	Weekdays	Extended Mondays to Saturdays from Tulse Hill (Tulse Hill Hotel) to West Norwood (Thurlow Arms) via Norwood Road.
09.09.1912	**93**	Daily	New Route: Bow Road Station (Und.) – Romford (Gidea Park, Unicorn) via Bow Road, Stratford High Street, Stratford Broadway, Romford Road, Ilford Hill, Ilford High Road, High Road Seven Kings, High Road Goodmayes, High Road Chadwell Heath, London Road, High Street Romford, Romford Market Place, Main Road.
.10.1912(?)	**89**	Sundays	Route withdrawn.
04.10.1912	**43**	Daily	*Associated Omnibus Company buses operated by L.G.O.C. on this route and others – see note in section (b) under this company heading.*
05.10.1912	**11**	Daily	Last day of operation on Mondays to Saturdays between Wormwood Scrubs and Hammersmith (see Route 72).
06.10.1912	**11**	Daily	Last day of operation on Sundays between Wormwood Scrubs and Shepherds Bush (Bush Hotel) (see Route 72).
06.10.1912	**30**	Daily	Last day of operation on Sundays between Putney Station and Twickenham Station.
07.10.1912			*Willesden garage (AC) opened.*
07.10.1912	**18**	Daily	Withdrawn between Ludgate Circus and Clapham Common (Plough) (see Route 45) and re-routed daily to operate to London Bridge Station via Ludgate Hill, St. Paul's Churchyard, Cannon Street, King William Street, London Bridge. Also re-routed between Holborn and Ludgate Circus via St. Andrew Street, Shoe Lane, St. Bride Street instead of Charterhouse Street, Farringdon Street.
07.10.1912	**21**	Daily	Withdrawn between London Street* and Greenwich Park (Gloucester) and re-routed daily to operate to Greenwich (Tunnel Avenue) via Nelson Street*, Romney Road, Trafalgar Road, Woolwich Road.
07.10.1912	**27**	Daily	Withdrawn between Islington Green and Stoke Newington (Birdcage) and re-routed daily to operate to Highbury Station via Upper Street. (See 65).

| 07.10.1912 | **44** | Daily | Withdrawn between Putney Bridge and Putney Station and re-routed daily to operate to Putney Common (Cricketers) via Windsor Street*, Lower Richmond Road. |

| 07.10.1912 | **45** | Daily | New Route: (See Route 18) South Hampstead (Swiss Cottage) – Clapham Common Station (Und.) via Adelaide Road, Chalk Farm Road, Camden Town High Street*, Crowndale Road, Pancras Road, Euston Road, Grays Inn Road, Holborn, Holborn Circus, Charterhouse Street, Farringdon Street, New Bridge Street, Blackfriars Bridge, Blackfriars Road, London Road, Elephant & Castle, Walworth Road*, Camberwell Road, Camberwell Green, Denmark Hill, Coldharbour Lane, Gresham Road, Brixton Road, Acre Lane, Clapham Park Road. |

| 07.10.1912 | **60** | Sundays | Re-routed in Harrow to serve Harrow on the Hill Station (Metropolitan Railway). |

| 07.10.1912 | **65** | Daily | New Route: (See Route 27) Stoke Newington (Birdcage) – Brompton Oratory via Stamford Hill, Stoke Newington High Street, Church Street, Albion Road, Newington Green, Newington Green Road, Essex Road, Upper Street, Islington High Street, Pentonville Road, Euston Road, Marylebone Road, Baker Street, Portman Square, Orchard Street, Oxford Street, Marble Arch, Park Lane, Hamilton Place, Hyde Park Corner, Knightsbridge, Brompton Road. |

| 07.10.1912 | **70** | Daily | New Route: Kensal Rise Station – South Hackney (Alexandra Hotel) via Station Road*, Chamberlayne Road, Kilburn Lane, Canterbury Road*, Malvern Road*, Shirland Road, Formosa Street, Warwick Avenue, Clifton Gardens, Maida Vale, Edgware Road, Marble Arch, Oxford Street, Regent Street, Piccadilly Circus, Haymarket, Cockspur Street, Trafalgar Square (south side), Strand, Fleet Street, Ludgate Hill, St. Paul's Churchyard, Cannon Street, Queen Victoria Street, Bank, Threadneedle Street, Bishopsgate, Norton Folgate, Shoreditch High Street, Hackney Road, Cambridge Road*, Victoria Park Road. |

| 07.10.1912 | **72** | Daily | New Route: (see Route 11) Liverpool Street Station – Wormwood Scrubs via New Broad Street*, Old Broad Street, Threadneedle Street (return via Princes Street, Moorgate Street*, London Wall, Blomfield Street, Liverpool Street), Bank, Queen Victoria Street, Cannon Street, St. Paul's Churchyard, Ludgate Hill, Fleet Street, Strand, Charing Cross, Whitehall, Parliament Street, Parliament Square, Broad Sanctuary, Victoria Street, Buckingham Palace Road, Pimlico Road, Lower Sloane Street, Sloane Square, Kings Road, Harwood Road, The Broadway Walham Green*, Dawes Road, Crown Road*, Fulham Palace Road, Queen Street*, Hammersmith Broadway, Brook Green Road*, Shepherds Bush Road, The Lawn*, Wood Lane. |

| 13.10.1912 | **38** | Daily | Withdrawn on Sundays between Leyton (Bakers' Arms) and Epping Forest (Rising Sun) and re-routed on Sundays at Leyton (Bakers' Arms) to operate to Leyton Green as on Mondays to Saturdays. |

| 21.10.1912 | **28** | Daily | Extended daily from West Hampstead (West End Green) to Golders Green Station via Fortune Green Road, Finchley Road. |

| 31.10.1912 | **31** | Daily | Withdrawn between Belsize Road and Finchley Road Station (Met.) and re-routed daily to Gospel Oak (Mansfield) via Eton Avenue, Englands Lane, Parkhill Road, Fleet Road. |

| 31.10.1912 | **93** | Daily | Extended daily from Bow Road Station (Und.) to operate from Mile End Station (Und.) via Bow Road and line of route. |

| 04.11.1912 | **82** | Daily | Withdrawn between Hounslow Barracks Station (Und.)* and the junction of Wellington Road and Staines Road and re-routed daily to operate from Heston-Hounslow Station (Und.)* via Lampton Road, Staines Road. |

09.11.1912	**86**	Daily	Last day of operation between Cranbrook Park (Beehive Lane) and Barkingside (Maypole).
14.11.1912	**62**	Daily	New Route: Highgate (Archway Tavern) – Waterloo Station via Holloway Road, Camden Road, Caledonian Road, Kings Cross Road, Farringdon Road, Farringdon Street, New Bridge Street, Blackfriars Bridge, Stamford Street.
20.11.1912	**49**	Daily	Last day of operation between Camden Town Station (Und.) and Kensington (Church Street*). (See Route 74).
21.11.1912	**69**	Daily	New Route: Poplar (Blackwall Tunnel) – Plumstead (Orchard Road, Rose & Crown) via Blackwall Tunnel, Tunnel Avenue, Woolwich Road, Albion Road*, George Street*, Church Street*, High Street Woolwich, Market Hill, Beresford Street (return via Powis Street, Parsons Hill*), Beresford Square, Plumstead Road, Plumstead High Street.
21.11.1912	**74**	Daily	New Route: Camden Town Station (Und.) – Kensington Gardens via Park Street*, Albert Road*, St. John's Wood Road, Grove Road, Lisson Grove, Marylebone Road*, Chapel Street, Praed Street, Eastbourne Terrace, Bishop's Road*, Queens Road*. (See Route 49). *(Proof tickets dated June 1912 show this route had originally been allocated the number 42 with an intended terminus of Queens Road Station).*
24.11.1912	**54**	Sundays	Last day of operation.
28.11.1912	**76**	Daily	New Route: Victoria Station – Stoke Newington (Weavers' Arms) via Wilton Road (return via Buckingham Palace Road), Victoria Street, Broad Sanctuary, Parliament Square, Bridge Street, Westminster Bridge, York Road, Stamford Street, Blackfriars Bridge, Queen Victoria Street, Bank, Threadneedle Street, Bishopsgate, Norton Folgate, Shoreditch High Street, Kingsland Road, Kingsland High Street, Stoke Newington Road, Stoke Newington High Street. *(This route replaced a horse bus route which had been running since 1880 between Liverpool Street and Waterloo which was the only route operated by the Railways & Metropolitan Omnibus Co.)*
30.11.1912	**17**	Daily	Last day of operation on Mondays to Saturdays between South Ealing (New Inn) and Ealing Broadway (Railway Hotel). (See Route 91).
.12.1912	**27**	Daily	Re-routed daily between High Street Notting Hill Gate* and Marylebone Road via Bayswater Road, Lancaster Gate Terrace*, Sussex Gardens, Grand Junction Road (Oxford and Cambridge Terrace)*, Marylebone Road* to Marylebone Road and line of route instead of via Pembridge Villas, Westbourne Grove, Bishop's Road*, Eastbourne Terrace, Praed Street, Chapel Street.
01.12.1912	**23**	Daily	Last day of operation on Sundays between South Ealing (New Inn) and Ealing Broadway (Railway Hotel). (See Route 91).
01.12.1912	**52**	Sundays	Last day of operation. (Re-introduced 21.03.1913 and renumbered 104).
01.12.1912	**57**	Sundays	Last day of operation.
01.12.1912	**58**	Sundays	Last day of operation. (Re-introduced 21.03.1913 and renumbered 102).
01.12.1912	**60**	Sundays	Last day of operation.
02.12.1912	**35A**	Daily	New Route: Elephant & Castle – Walthamstow (Wood Street, Duke's Head) via Newington Causeway, Borough High Street, London Bridge, King William Street, Gracechurch Street, Bishopsgate, Norton Folgate, Shoreditch High Street, Kingsland Road, Dalston Lane, Pembury Road, Cricketfield Road, Downs Road, Lower Clapton Road, Lea Bridge Road, Hoe Street, Forest Road, Wood Street.

02.12.1912	**67**	Daily	New Route: Leyton (Bakers' Arms) – Poplar (Blackwall Tunnel) via Leyton High Road, Major Road, Chobham Road, Leyton Road, Angel Lane, Great Eastern Road, The Grove, Stratford Broadway, West Ham Lane, Church Street, Plaistow Road, High Street Plaistow, Balaam Street, Barking Road, East India Dock Road.
02.12.1912	**91**	Daily	New Route: Ealing Broadway Station – Kew Bridge (Star & Garter) via Ealing Broadway, Ealing High Street, St. Mary's Road, Ealing Road*, Brentford High Street, Kew Bridge Road.
07.12.1912	**48**	Daily	Extended daily from Stockwell (Swan) to Merton (Pincott Road, Nelson Arms) via Clapham Road, Clapham High Street, Clapham Common (south side), Balham Hill, Balham High Road, Upper Tooting Road, Tooting High Street, High Street Colliers Wood, High Street Merton.
08.12.1912	**2**	Daily	Last day of operation between Finchley Road Station (Met.) and Golders Green Station
09.12.1912	**84**	Sats & Suns	Introduced on Mondays to Fridays between Golders Green Station and St. Albans (Rising Sun) as on Saturdays and Sundays.
12.12.1912	**37**	Daily	Extended daily from Isleworth (Northumberland Arms) to Hounslow (Star) via South Street, St. John's Road, Loring Road, Linkfield Road, London Road.
12.12.1912	**59**	Sundays	Introduced on Mondays to Saturdays between Oxford Circus and South Croydon (Red Deer) via existing Sunday route.
12.12.1912	**65**	Daily	Extended daily from Brompton Oratory to Fulham (Salisbury) via Thurloe Place, Onslow Square, Sydney Place, Fulham Road, The Broadway Walham Green*, Dawes Road.
15.12.1912	**75**	Daily	New Route: Woolwich (Crown & Anchor) – South Croydon (Swan & Sugar Loaf) via Hare Street, Powis Street (return via Beresford Square, Beresford Street, Market Hill), Greens End, Wellington Street, Artillery Place, Hill Street*, Little Heath, Charlton Road*, Vanbrugh Park, Charlton Road*, unnamed road across Blackheath*, Montpelier Row, Montpelier Vale, (return via Tranquil Vale, Royal Parade), Tranquil Vale*, Lee Road*, Lee Green, Burnt Ash Road, Newstead Road*, Birch Grove, St. Mildred's Road, Brownhill Road, Rushey Green, Catford Road, Catford Hill, Perry Hill, Bell Green, Sydenham Road, Newlands Park, Lennard Road, Parish Lane, Green Lane, Croydon Road, Penge Road, High Street Norwood, Selhurst Road, Northcote Road, Whitehorse Road, St. James's Road, Oakfield Road, London Road, North End, High Street Croydon, South End, Brighton Road. *Operated by Thomas Tilling Ltd.*
19.12.1912	**88**	Daily	Last day of operation. (See Route 87).
19.12.1912	**28**	Daily	Last day of operation between Childs Hill (Castle) and Golders Green Station.
19.12.1912	**31**	Daily	Last day of operation between South Hampstead (Swiss Cottage) and Gospel Oak (Mansfield).
20.12.1912	**28**	Daily	Re-routed daily between North End Road and Kensington Road* via Matheson Road*, Avonmore Road, Hammersmith Road instead of Lillie Road, Richmond Road*, Earls Court Road.

20.12.1912	**49**	Daily	Extended daily from Kensington (Church Street*) to operate from Shepherds Bush (Bush Hotel) via Uxbridge Road, Holland Road, Kensington Road*, Kensington High Street to Kensington Road and line of route. Also extended daily from Clapham Junction to Streatham Common (Greyhound) via St .John's Road, Northcote Road, Montholme Road, Thurleigh Road*, Nightingale Lane, Bellevue Road, Trinity Road, Tooting Bec Road, Tooting Bec Gardens, Streatham High Road.
20.12.1912	**77**	Daily	New Route: Kings Cross Station – East Hill (French Horn & Half Moon) via Euston Road, Upper Woburn Place, Tavistock Square (east side), Woburn Place, Russell Square (east side), Southampton Row, Kingsway, Aldwych (western arm), Strand, Charing Cross, Whitehall, Parliament Street, Bridge Street, Westminster Bridge, Stangate*, Lambeth Palace Road*, Albert Embankment, Wandsworth Road, Lavender Hill, St. John's Hill, East Hill (turn via Woodwell Street, Huguenot Place back to East Hill).
20.12.1912	**87**	Daily	Extended daily from Highgate (Archway Tavern) to Clapton Pond via Holloway Road, Seven Sisters Road, Blackstock Road, Brownswood Road, Lordship Park, Manor Road, Stamford Hill, Northwold Road, Upper Clapton Road. (See Route 88).
30.12.1912	**9A**	Weekdays	New Route: Hammersmith Broadway – Piccadilly Circus via Hammersmith Road, Kensington Road*, Kensington High Street, Kensington Road, Kensington Gore, Knightsbridge, Hyde Park Corner, Piccadilly.

(b)   Other Operators

(i)   Associated Omnibus Company Ltd.

This company, founded in 1900 to acquire horse bus operations, had worked in various associations. Motor bus operations commenced in 1905 (see Volume 1, page 7). They withdrew all motor buses in July 1907 and concentrated on horse buses. They took over several routes by arrangement with L.G.O.C. and Tillings when they withdrew. In 1912 it was decided to resume motor bus operation and an agreement was reached with the L.G.O.C. dated 25.08.1912 by which Associated purchased 55 B type buses from L.G.O.C., who undertook to work them on agreed terms as part of the pool. The buses were allocated to L.G.O.C. garages, the first being Holloway (J) and the first route being 43. Associated routes are included but not differentiated in the L.G.O.C. sections.

(ii)   London and North Western Railway Company

01.10.1912		Weekdays	Additional Service introduced: Watford Junction Station – Roxborough Bridge (Roxborough Hotel) via Clarendon Road, Watford High Street, Lower High Street, Pinner Road, Aldenham Road, Chalk Hill, London Road, High Street Bushey, Sparrows Herne, High Road Bushey Heath, Common Road, Brooks Hill, Chapel Hill Road*, High Road Harrow Weald, Wealdstone High Street, Station Road, St. Ann's Road*, Springfield Road*, Kymberley Road, Headstone Road, College Road.

(iii)   Metropolitan Steam Omnibus Company Ltd.

By July 1912 this company owned some 60 buses (of which only 42 were actually in service) using the French Darracq-Serpollet motor, which the manufacturers ceased to produce, nor could spares be obtained. The company decided therefore to change to using petrol engined buses.

29.09.1912		Daily	Last day of operation of the Petersham (Dysart Arms) – Brixton (Lambeth Town Hall) route.
15.10.1912		Daily	Last day of operation of the Fulham (Salisbury) – Gipsy Hill (Paxton) route.

| 16.10.1912 | *Agreement signed with L.G.O.C. to provide up to 100 B type buses in Metropolitan Steam livery and operate them on L.G.O.C. routes on behalf of Metropolitan Steam as part of the London pool. First three B type were operated from Willesden garage (AC). By 31.12.1912 85 B type were in service on Routes 6,8,18,66 and after March 1913 on Route 46. The 100 B type were all in service by 27.01.1913. From hereon Metropolitan Steam routes are included but not differentiated in the L.G.O.C. sections.* |

(iv) National Steam Car Company

.10.1912(?)	Sundays	Peckham Rye (King's Arms) – Kew Green route withdrawn.
.10.1912(?)	Sundays	Stratford Broadway – Peckham Rye (King's Arms) route withdrawn. It is surmised that the Liverpool Street Station – Peckham (Rye Lane) route became daily thereafter.
.10.1912(?)	Sundays	It is assumed that the Oxford Circus – Bexley (King's Head) route was withdrawn for the winter.
.10.1912(?)	Sundays	It is assumed that the Peckham Rye (King's Arms) – Hampton Court route was withdrawn for the winter.
18.11.1912	Daily	New Route: St. John's Wood (Eyre Arms) – Peckham Rye (King's Arms) via Grove End Road, Grove Road, Lisson Grove, Marylebone Road, York Place*, Baker Street, Portman Square (east side), Orchard Street, Oxford Street, New Oxford Street, High Holborn, Holborn, Holborn Viaduct, Newgate Street, Cheapside, Bank, King William Street, London Bridge, Borough High Street, Newington Causeway, Elephant & Castle, Walworth Road*, Camberwell Road, Camberwell Green, Church Street*, Peckham Road, Peckham High Street, Rye Lane.
20.12.1912	Daily	St. John's Wood (Eyre Arms) – Peckham Rye (King's Arms) route re-routed daily between Oxford Circus and Elephant & Castle via Regent Street, Piccadilly Circus, Lower Regent Street, Waterloo Place, Pall Mall, Cockspur Street, Whitehall, Parliament Street, Bridge Street, Westminster Bridge, Westminster Bridge Road, St. George's Road to Elephant & Castle and line of route.

(v) New Central Omnibus Company Ltd.

?.10.1912(?)	Sundays	Waterloo Station – Hampton Court route withdrawn.
?. ?.1912	Weekdays	Richmond – Thames Ditton (Angel) route withdrawn between Surbiton Station and Thames Ditton (Angel).
?. ?.1912	Sundays	Kew Bridge – Thames Ditton (Angel) route withdrawn between Kew Bridge and Richmond and between Surbiton Station and Thames Ditton (Angel).

(vi) Tramways (M.E.T.) Omnibus Company Ltd.

The origin of this company has been fully recorded in many publications. It became part of the Underground-L.G.O.C. combine in 1912 and under the agreement, all its buses were operated by the L.G.O.C. on their routes, commencing in January 1913 (see Volume 3).

MOTOR OMNIBUS ROUTES AS AT TUESDAY 31ST DECEMBER 1912

(a) L.G.O.C. & Thomas Tilling Ltd.

1	Mons-Fris &Sats a.m.	West Hendon (Station Road) – Tower Bridge (Tooley Street)
	Sats p.m. & Suns	Edgware (Royal Oak) – Tower Bridge (Tooley Street)

2	Daily	Ebury Bridge (Monster) – Finchley Road Station (Met.)
3	Weekdays	Brixton (George Canning) – Camden Town Station (Und.)
4	Daily	Finsbury Park Station – Elephant & Castle
5	Weekdays	Stroud Green (Stapleton Hall Tavern) – Putney Station
	Sundays	Stroud Green (Stapleton Hall Tavern) – Wimbledon (Rose & Crown)
6	Weekdays	Kensal Rise Station – Shoreditch Church
	Sundays	Kensal Rise Station – Charing Cross (Trafalgar Square)
7	Daily	Wormwood Scrubs – Liverpool Street Station
8	Daily	Willesden (White Horse) – Old Ford (Lady Franklin)
9	Daily	Barnes (Avondale Road) – Liverpool Street Station
9A	Weekdays	Hammersmith Broadway – Piccadilly Circus
10	Daily	Wanstead (George) – Elephant & Castle
11	Weekdays	Hammersmith – Liverpool Street Station
	Sundays	Shepherds Bush (Bush Hotel) – Liverpool Street Station
12	Daily	Turnham Green Church – Peckham Rye (King's Arms)
		Joint operation by Thomas Tilling Ltd. & L.G.O.C. on weekdays. L.G.O.C. only on Sundays.
13	Weekdays	London Bridge Station – Hendon (Bell)
	Sundays	Charing Cross (Trafalgar Square) – Hendon (Bell)
14	Daily	Hornsey Rise (Favourite) – Putney Station
15	Weekdays	Putney Common (Cricketers) – East Ham (Duke's Head)
	Sundays	Putney Common (Cricketers) – Plaistow (Abbey Arms)
16	Daily	Victoria Station – Cricklewood (Crown)
17	Weekdays	Ealing Broadway (Railway Hotel) – London Bridge Station
	Sundays	Ealing Broadway (Railway Hotel) – East Ham (Duke's Head)
18	Daily	Willesden (White Hart) – London Bridge Station
19	Daily	Clapham Junction (Northcote) – Highbury Barn
20	Daily	Shepherds Bush (Bush Hotel) – West Norwood (Rosendale)
21	Daily	Wood Green (Fishmongers' Arms) – Greenwich (Tunnel Avenue)
22	Weekdays	Homerton (Clapton Park Tavern) – Putney Station
23	Weekdays	Acton Vale (King's Arms) – Barking (Westbury)
	Sundays	Ealing Broadway (Railway Hotel) – Rippleside (Ship & Shovel)
24	Daily	Hampstead Heath (South End Green) – Pimlico (Gun)
25	Daily	Victoria Station – Seven Kings (Seven Kings Hotel)
26	Daily	West Kilburn (Falcon) – Hackney Wick
27	Daily	Twickenham Station – Highbury Station
28	Daily	Wandsworth Bridge (Tavern) – Childs Hill (Castle)

29	Weekdays	Victoria Station – Southgate (Cherry Tree)
	Sundays	Victoria Station – Hadley Woods (Cock Inn)

30	Daily	Kings Cross Station – Putney Station

31	Daily	Chelsea (Stanley Arms) – South Hampstead (Swiss Cottage)

32	Weekdays	Charing Cross (Trafalgar Square) – Ladbroke Grove (Eagle)

33	Weekdays	Liverpool Street Station – East Sheen (Black Horse)
	Sundays	Piccadilly Circus – East Sheen (Black Horse)

34	Weekdays	Liverpool Street Station – West Norwood (Thurlow Arms)

35	Weekdays	Elephant & Castle – Walthamstow (Crooked Billet)
	Sundays	Brixton (George Canning) – Chingford Mount (Prince Albert)

35A	Daily	Elephant & Castle – Walthamstow (Duke's Head)

36	Daily	West Kilburn (Falcon) – Catford (St. Laurence Church)
		Joint operation by Thomas Tilling Ltd. on weekdays. L.G.O.C. only on Sundays.

37	Daily	Herne Hill (Half Moon Hotel) – Hounslow (Star)

38	Daily	Victoria Station – Leyton Green

39	Daily	Victoria Station – Sidcup (Black Horse)
		Joint operation by Thomas Tilling Ltd.& L.G.O.C. on weekdays. L.G.O.C. only on Sundays

40	Daily	Elephant & Castle – Upton Park (Duke of Edinburgh)

41	Weekdays	Tufnell Park (Tufnell Park Hotel) – Old Ford (Lady Franklin)

42	Daily	Finsbury Park Station – Tower of London

43	Daily	Muswell Hill Broadway – London Bridge Station

44	Daily	Highgate (Archway Tavern) – Putney Common (Cricketers)

45	Daily	South Hampstead (Swiss Cottage) – Clapham Common Station (Und.)

46	Weekdays	Victoria Station – Kilburn Station (L.&N.W.R.)

47	Daily	Shoreditch Church – Bromley (Market Place)
		Operated by Thomas Tilling Ltd.

48	Daily	Tottenham (Swan) – Merton (Nelson Arms)

49	Daily	Shepherds Bush (Bush Hotel) – Streatham Common (Greyhound)

50	Weekdays	Shepherds Bush (Bush Hotel) – Liverpool Street Station

51	Sundays	Somerset House – Hampton Court via Putney, Richmond and Kingston

52		*Number not in use*

53	Sundays	North Finchley (Swan & Pyramids) – Ebury Bridge (Monster)

54		*Number not in use*

55	Sats & Suns	Elephant & Castle – Buckhurst Hill (Bald Faced Stag)

56	Sundays	Elephant & Castle – Epping Forest (Warren Wood House)

57 – 58		*Numbers not in use*
59	Weekdays	Oxford Circus – South Croydon (Red Deer)
	Sundays	Camden Town Station (Und.) – South Croydon (Red Deer)
60		*Number not in use*
61	Sundays	Brixton (White Horse) – Whyteleafe (Tavern)
62	Daily	Highgate (Archway Tavern) – Waterloo Station
63	Sundays	Sidcup (Black Horse) – Oxford Circus
		Operated by Thomas Tilling Ltd.
64	Sundays	Bromley (Market Place) – Oxford Circus
		Operated by Thomas Tilling Ltd.
65	Daily	Stoke Newington (Birdcage) – Fulham (Salisbury)
66	Daily	Willesden (Pound Lane) – Tooting (Mitre)
67	Daily	Leyton (Bakers' Arms) – Poplar (Blackwall Tunnel)
68		*Number not in use*
69	Daily	Poplar (Blackwall Tunnel) – Plumstead (Orchard Road, Rose & Crown)
70	Daily	Kensal Rise Station – South Hackney (Alexandra Hotel)
71		*Number not in use*
72	Daily	Liverpool Street Station – Wormwood Scrubs
73		*Number not in use*
74	Daily	Camden Town Station (Und.) – Kensington Gardens
75	Daily	Woolwich (Crown & Anchor) – South Croydon (Swan & Sugar Loaf)
		Operated by Thomas Tilling Ltd.
76	Daily	Victoria Station – Stoke Newington (Weavers' Arms)
77	Daily	Kings Cross Station – East Hill (French Horn & Half Moon)
78 – 79		*Numbers not in use*
80	Daily	Ealing Broadway Station – Northfields (Plough)
81	Daily	Hounslow (Bell) – Windsor Castle
82	Daily	Heston-Hounslow Station* – Staines (Police Station)
83	Daily	Golders Green Station – West Hendon (Station Road)
84	Daily	Golders Green Station – St. Albans (Rising Sun)
85	Weekdays	Putney Bridge Station – Roehampton (Earl Spencer)
	Sundays	Putney Bridge Station – Kingston Hill (Tram Terminus)
86	Daily	Barking Station – Cranbrook Park (Beehive Lane)
87	Daily	Colney Hatch Lane (Wilton Road) – Clapton Pond

88 – 90   *Numbers not in use*

91   Daily   Ealing Broadway Station – Kew Bridge (Star & Garter)

92   *Number not in use*

93   Daily   Mile End Station (Und.) – Romford (Gidea Park, Unicorn)

(b)   Other Operators

(i)   British Automobile Development Ltd. ('British')

Daily   Liverpool Street Station – Victoria Station

(ii)   London and North Western Railway Company

Weekdays   North Watford (Callowlands, Buckingham Road) – Croxley Green (Yorke Road)

Weekdays   Watford Junction Station – Harrow & Wealdstone Station

Weekdays   Harrow & Wealdstone Station – Harrow (Post Office)

Weekdays   Watford Junction Station – Roxborough Bridge (Roxborough Hotel)

(iii)   National Steam Car Company

Daily   Shepherds Bush (White Horse) – Peckham Rye (King's Arms)

Weekdays   Shepherds Bush (Victoria Tavern) – Liverpool Street Station

Daily   Fulham (Salisbury) – Liverpool Street Station

Daily(?)   Liverpool Street Station – Peckham (Rye Lane)

Daily(?)   Chalk Farm (Adelaide) – Peckham Rye (King's Arms)

Daily   St. John's Wood (Eyre Arms) – Peckham Rye (King's Arms)

(iv)   New Central Omnibus Company Ltd.

Daily   Chalk Farm (Adelaide) – Camberwell Green

Daily   Richmond Station – Surbiton Station

Daily   Kingston (Market Place) – Esher (Bear)

(v)   Park Langley Estate

Daily (?)   Beckenham Junction Station – Park Langley Estate (Whitecroft Way) *(residents only)*
Operated under contract by H.Taylor of Beckenham.

****

APPENDIX – ROAD NAMES etc. WHICH HAVE CHANGED
(Marked in the route lists with an asterisk)
Note that this incorporates our latest research into name changes and in some instances items are included here for the first time which should have appeared in previously published volumes.

Name in 1908-1912	Current Name
Albert Road (by Zoological Gardens)	Prince Albert Road
Albion Road	Woolwich Church Street (part of)
Archer Street	Westbourne Grove (part of)
Barnes Terrace	The Terrace
Bath Road (section east of Colnbrook High Street)	Park Street, Bridge Street
Bath Road (section west of Crown Close, Colnbrook)	London Road
Beeches Road (section running north-south)	Green Lane
Bishops Road	Bishops Bridge Road
Bishopsgate Street	Bishopsgate (renamed on 01.01.1911)
Bridport Place	Section no longer exists
Bromley Road (Downham) (part of)	Old Bromley Road
Brook Green Road	Shepherds Bush Road (part of)
Cambridge Park (western section)	Cambridge Park Road
Cambridge Road (Bethnal Green)	Cambridge Heath Road
Cambridge Road (Kilburn Park)	Sections no longer exist
Camden Town High Street	Camden High Street
Canterbury Road (western section)	Carlton Vale (part of)
Chapel Hill Road	High Road Harrow Weald (part of)
Charlton Road (section by Greenwich Park)	Charlton Way
Charlton Road (section east of Charlton Church Lane)	The Village, Charlton Park Road
Church Street (Camberwell)	Camberwell Church Street
Church Street (Kensington)	Kensington Church Street
Church Street (Woolwich)	Woolwich Church Street (part of)
Colney Hatch Lane (section south of Muswell Road)	Muswell Hill Broadway (part of)
Commercial Road East	Commercial Road
Cornwall Road	Westbourne Park Road (part of)
Cranley Terrace	Onslow Square (part of)
Crown Road	Lillie Road (part of)
Defoe Road	Garratt Lane (part of)
Dockhead (western section)	Jamaica Road (part of)
Ealing Road (section north of Whitestile Road)	South Ealing Road
Earl Street	Marsham Street (part of)
East Burnham Road	Hawthorn Lane
Edgware Road (section between Montrose Avenue and Deansbrook Road)	Burnt Oak Broadway
Edgware Road (section north of Edgware High Street)	Stone Grove
Edgware Road (section north of Kingsbury Road)	The Hyde
Foots Cray Road (section east of the Sidcup By Pass)	Main Road
Fortis Green Road (section from Tetherdown to East Finchley)	Fortis Green
George Street	Woolwich Church Street (part of)
Glasgow Terrace	This section no longer exists
Goldhawk Road (section on the south side of Shepherds Bush Green)	Shepherds Bush Green (south side) *NOTE: The section of road east of the Green was Uxbridge Road to the junction of Holland Park Avenue/Norland Road but in the route listings this is ignored to avoid confusion with the north side of Shepherds Bush Green.*
Grand Junction Road (Oxford and Cambridge Terrace)	Sussex Gardens (part of)
Green Street (Bethnal Green)	Roman Road (part of)
Greenwich Road	Greenwich High Road (part of)
Grosvenor Road (between Lambeth & Vauxhall Bridges)	Millbank (part of)
Harrow Road (section north of Craven Park)	Hillside, Brentfield
Hart Street	Bloomsbury Way
Heston Hounslow Station (Und.)	Hounslow Central Station (Und.)
High Street Notting Hill Gate	Notting Hill Gate

Name in 1908-1912	Current Name
Hill Street (Woolwich Common)	Hill Reach
Hounslow Barracks Station (Und.)	Hounslow West Station (Und.)
Kensington Road (section west of Kensington High Street)	Kensington High Street (part of)
King William Street (Greenwich)	King William Walk
Lambeth Palace Road (northern section)	Substantially realigned
Lancaster Gate Terrace	Lancaster Terrace
Lee Road (section north of Lee Terrace)	Blackheath Village (part of)
Lewisham High Road	Lewisham Way
London Street	Greenwich High Road (part of)
Longbridge Road (western section)	Station Parade
Lower Road (Richmond)	Petersham Road
Malvern Road (northern section)	Carlton Vale (part of) and section no longer exists
Marylebone Road (western end between Cosway Street and Edgware Road)	Old Marylebone Road
Matheson Road (western end)	North End Crescent, Stanwick Road
Montpelier Road West	Montpelier Avenue
Moorgate Street	Moorgate
Muswell Hill Road (section north of Fortis Green Road)	Muswell Hill Broadway (part of)
Nelson Street	Nelson Road
New Broad Street (section between Liverpool Street & Wormwood Street)	Old Broad Street (part of)
New Road (Barnet)	St. Albans Road and section at Bignell's Corner no longer exists
Newington Butts (section north of Draper Street)	Elephant & Castle
Newstead Road (eastern section)	No longer exists (Kimbolton Close follows line)
Northfield Lane	Northfield Avenue
Oakley Street	Baylis Road
Park Street	Parkway
Parker's Row (eastern section)	Jamaica Road (part of)
Parsons Hill	John Wilson Street (part of)
Portsmouth Road (northern section at Putney Heath)	Wildcroft Road (part of)
Putney Heath (east side)	Tibbet's Ride
Queen Street (Hammersmith)	Queen Caroline Street
Queens Road (Bayswater)	Queensway
Richmond Road (Bayswater)	Chepstow Road
Richmond Road (Kingston)(section south of Cromwell Road)	Clarence Street (part of)
Richmond Road (Shepherds Bush)	Richmond Way
Richmond Road (West Brompton)	Old Brompton Road (part of)
St. Ann's Road (Harrow)	Section no longer exists
St. Margaret's Road (northern section)	Richmond Road
Seymour Street	Eversholt Street (part of)
Shacklegate Road	Shacklegate Lane
Silver Street (Greenwich)	Nevada Street
Springfield Road	Section no longer exists
Stangate	No longer exists
Stanmore New Road	London Road
Station Road (Kensal Rise)	Station Terrace
The Broadway, Walham Green	Fulham Broadway
The Lawn (Shepherds Bush)	Shepherds Bush Green (west side)
Thurleigh Road (eastern link to Nightingale Lane)	Thurleigh Avenue
Tranquil Vale (section south of Montpelier Vale)	Blackheath Village (part of)
Union Road	Jamaica Road (part of)
Unnamed road across Blackheath	Prince Charles Road
Upper Baker Street	Baker Street (part of)
Walworth Road (section north of Draper Street)	Elephant & Castle
Warwick Street	Warwick Way
Water Lane	Brixton Water Lane
Wellington Street (section south of Strand)	Lancaster Place
Victoria Road	Foots Cray Road (part of)

Name in 1908-1912	Current Name
Windsor Street	Lower Richmond Road (part of)
York Place	Baker Street (part of)
York Road	York Way

SELECTIVE BIBLIOGRAPHY

BARKER, Theo
  Moving millions – a pictorial history of London Transport. *London Transport Museum, 1990*
BARKER, T.C. & ROBBINS, M.:
  A history of London Transport – Volume 2: The twentieth century to 1970. *Allen & Unwin, 1974*
CRAWLEY, R.J. and others:
  The years between 1909-1969 – Volume 1: The National story to 1929. *D.R.MacGregor, 1979*
DAY, John R.:
  The story of the London bus: London and its buses from the horse bus to the present day.
                                                                London Transport, 1973
FULLER, K.:
  Radical aristocrats – London busworkers from the 1880s to the 1980s. *Lawrence & Wishart, 1985*
LEE, Charles.E.:
  The early motor bus. *British Transport Commission, 1962*
LONDON COUNTY COUNCIL:
  Names of streets and places in the Administrative County of London. *L.C.C. – various editions*
MORRIS, O.J. (Ed.)
  Fares please – the story of London's road transport *Ian Allan, 1953*
ROBBINS, G.J.:
  Metropolitan – the story of the Tramways (M.E.T.) Omnibus Company Limited. 1912-1933.
                                                                 Omnibus Society, n.d.
ROBBINS, G.J. & ATKINSON, J.B.:
  The London B-type motor omnibus – 3rd edition. *D.P.R.Marketing & Sales, 1991*
SCANLAN, H.D.:
  A lifetime of London bus work. *Transport Publishing Co., 1979*
SOMMERFIELD, Vernon:
  London's buses – the story of a hundred years. *The St. Catherine Press, 1933*
TAYLOR, Sheila (Ed.)
  A journey through time – London Transport photographs 1880 to 1965. *Laurence King, 1992*
  The moving Metropolis. A history of London's transport since 1800 *Laurence King, 2001*

Extensive research has been carried out in the Bus Maps issued by the London General Omnibus Company and in local newspapers during the period covered. Reference has also been made to many London street atlases.

❖❖❖❖❖❖❖❖❖❖❖

LONDON GENERAL OMNIBUS COMPANY Ltd.

MAP OF OMNIBUS SERVICES – MARCH 1911

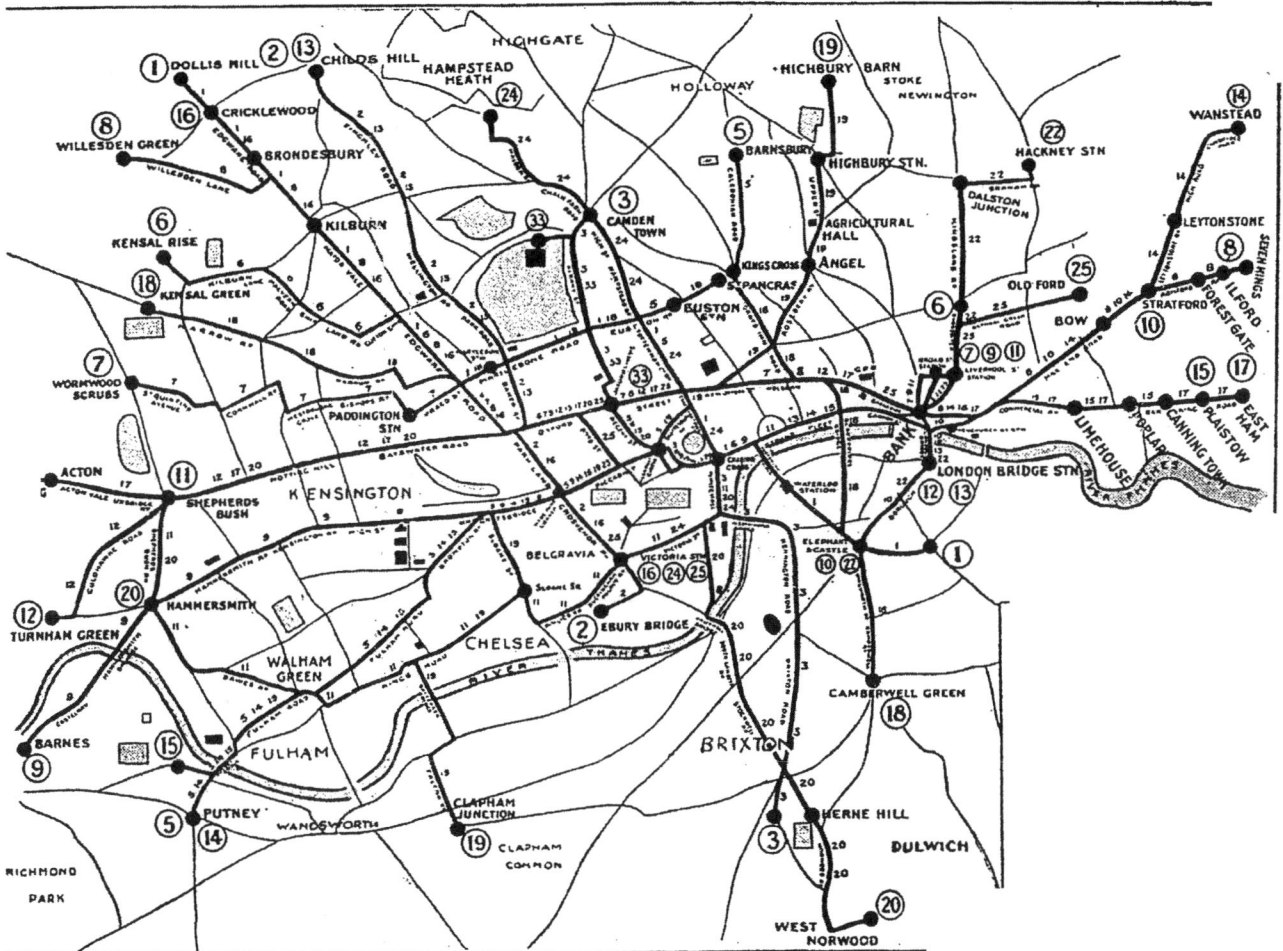

OPEN AIR
TO
EVERYWHERE
LIST OF MOTOR SERVICES
----

1. TOWER BRIDGE RD - DOLLIS HILL
2. CHILD'S HILL - EBURY BRIDGE
3. BRIXTON *(George Canning)* - CAMDEN TOWN
5. PUTNEY - BARNSBURY
6. KENSAL RISE - SHOREDITCH
7. LIVERPOOL STREET - WORMWOOD SCRUBS
8. WILLESDEN GREEN - SEVEN KINGS
9. LIVERPOOL STREET - BARNES
10. ELEPHANT & CASTLE - STRATFORD
11. SHEPHERD'S BUSH - LIVERPOOL STREET
12. LONDON BRIDGE STATION - TURNHAM GREEN
13. LONDON BRIDGE STATION - CHILD'S HILL
14. PUTNEY - WANSTEAD
15. PUTNEY COMMON - PLAISTOW
16. VICTORIA STATION - CRICKLEWOOD
17. EALING - EAST HAM
18. KENSAL GREEN - CAMBERWELL GREEN
19. CLAPHAM JUNCTION - HIGHBURY BARN
20. HAMMERSMITH - WEST NORWOOD
22. ELEPHANT & CASTLE - HACKNEY STATION
24. VICTORIA STATION - HAMPSTEAD HEATH
25. VICTORIA STATION - OLD FORD
33. OXFORD CIRCUS - ZOOLOGICAL GARDENS

Cover photographs

Front cover: London General Omnibus Company's X 2 stands ready for duty on Route 15 between Putney and Plaistow in December1909. Allocated to Farm Lane Garage, Fulham, which is the likely location of this photograph, it advertises Herbert Beerbohm Tree's intriguingly named Christmas offering at His Majesty's Theatre. *G.J. Robbins collection*

Rear cover (top): As explained on page 68, the LGOC operated B type buses on certain routes on behalf of the Associated Omnibus Company one of which was the 43 which to this day still operates between Muswell Hill and London Bridge Station although not via East Finchley as shown on the side route board which has been added to indicate the extension beyond the original terminus of Highgate (Archway Tavern). B 1917 stands in the yard of Holloway garage. *A.B. Cross from the G.J.Robbins collection*

Rear cover (bottom): A London Motor Omnibus Company Milnes Daimler on Route 6 to Kensal Rise overtakes one of the London Electrobus vehicles on the Liverpool Street to Victoria route which in turn is passing a rather weary looking goods horse. One is tempted to surmise that the slope of Fleet Street up from Ludgate Circus is proving a bit of a struggle for the battery operated vehicle encouraging the Milnes Daimler driver to prove his vehicle's strength. In the distance one of the remaining horse buses starts the climb and steam engines cross the bridge at the foot of Ludgate Hill. *D.A.Ruddom collection*